A series of student texts in

CONTEMPORARY BIOLOGY

General Editors:

Professor E. J. W. Barrington, F.R.S.
Professor Arthur J. Willis

The Biology of Fungi, Bacteria and Viruses

and Viruses

Second edition

Greta Stevenson
M.Sc.(Otago), Ph.D.(Lond.), D.I.C.

Edward Arnold (Publishers) Ltd., London

First published 1967
Second edition 1970

Boards SBN: 7131 2265 X
Paper SBN: 7131 2266 8

Printed in Great Britain by
William Clowes and Sons, Limited, London and Beccles

Preface

This book is intended for students in the early parts of their University courses in Botany and Biology and also for sixth-form pupils. It gives an introduction to the study of fungi, bacteria, viruses and other micro-organisms, a subject with many obvious and important economic applications, to which references are made. A single reading list is given to indicate directions in which the field may be explored more fully.

I am greatly indebted to Professor Lilian Hawker who most generously read the entire manuscript and made many helpful suggestions for its improvement. Miss Grace Waterhouse has also very kindly helped me and in presenting an up-to-date outline classification I have benefited from discussions with Dr. G. C. Ainsworth.

Many of the figures are original, others are taken from authors who are individually acknowledged. They are intended as a guide only to the *real living thing* which every student should endeavour to see for himself. For the shortcomings of the book I alone am responsible.

PREFACE TO THE SECOND EDITION

I am indebted to readers and reviewers who have pointed out errors and obscurities which, within the limits of the available space, I have endeavoured to correct. The section on viruses has been rewritten to give more detail, and at various other points in the book additional material has been incorporated. Four more plates are included, and I am indebted to the authors, who are acknowledged individually in the legends, who have generously given permission for the use of their electron micrographs and photographs illustrating some recent research. I am specially grateful to Professor A. J. Willis whose careful editing has meant so much to this revised edition as well as to the original book.

Winchester   Greta Stevenson
1970

Table of Contents

Tables

TABLE OF CONTRACTIONS

ADP	adenosine diphosphate
ATP	adenosine triphosphate
BHC	organic insecticide—benzenehexachloride
DDT	organic insecticide—dichlorophenyltrichloroethane
DNA	deoxyribonucleic acid
FAD	flavin adenine dinucleotide
IAA	indolyl acetic acid
NAD	nicotinamide adenine dinucleotide (DPN)
NADP	nicotinamide adenine dinucleotide phosphate (TPN)
RNA	ribonucleic acid
TMV	tobacco mosaic virus
2,4-D	dichlorophenoxyacetic acid

TABLE OF MEASUREMENTS

1 metre (m)	= 1,000 millimetres (mm)
1 millimetre	= 1,000 microns (μ)
1 micron	= 1,000 millimicrons (mμ)
1 millimicron	= 10 Ångstrøm units

TABLE OF COMPARATIVE SIZES

Object	Shape	Dimensions
Egg albumin protein molecule	ellipsoidal	2·5 × 10 mμ
Haemoglobin molecule	ellipsoidal	3 × 15 mμ
Foot and mouth disease virus	spheroidal	8–12 mμ
Tobacco necrosis virus	spheroidal	17 mμ

1*

Poliomyelitis virus	spheroidal	28 mμ
Tobacco mosaic virus	rod-shaped	300 × 15 mμ
Polyhedral viruses of insects	rod-shaped (but in polyhedral masses)	250–350 × 28–50 mμ
Virus of chicken pox and shingles	brick-shaped	290 × 230 mμ
Escherichia coli phage	{ head	95 × 65 mμ
	tail	100 × 25 mμ
Rickettsia spp.	ellipsoidal	350 × 250 mμ
Staphylococcus albus	spheroidal	1 μ
Mycobacterium tuberculosis	rod-shaped	2·5–3·5 × 0·3 μ
Salmonella typhi	rod-shaped	2–4 × 0·5 μ
Escherichia coli	rod-shaped	2–4 × 0·5 μ
Clostridium botulinum	rod-shaped	3–8 × 0·6–1 μ
Aspergillus niger conidium	spheroidal	2·5–4 μ
Botrytis cinerea conidium	ellipsoidal	8–12 × 6–10 μ

Introduction

In even the simplest scheme of naming and classifying living things the idea of relationships is inherent, an idea first fully developed by Darwin. So in general terms we take it for granted that the groups of organisms discussed in this book are more or less related to one another and to all other living organisms. Our present-day species are usually regarded, however, as the descendants and survivors of ancestral types of which we know very little, and probably modern forms represent only the twigs of a large and complex family tree of which we have but an incomplete outline (Fig. A.1, p. 176).

Fungi as we know them are far removed from the bacteria with which they may or may not be directly linked. Some show real or apparent similarities with algae of different families, and in the past were thought to be derived from them, but modern opinion ranks most fungi as a separate line of thallophyte development. The group Thallophyta is a convenient unit in classification whether its members are really related or not. It comprises the plants, algae and fungi, in which the plant body is a simple *thallus* showing no development of special vegetative organs such as the other groups of plants have. The Thallophyta presumably originated from unicellular organisms, but these show such diversity that the Thallophyta may well have arisen from various simpler groups, i.e. are polyphyletic in origin. The aquatic habit is considered more primitive than the terrestrial, and the aquatic fungi which produce motile cells are treated as the most primitive. The saprophytic habit (growing on dead organic matter) is regarded as simpler than the parasitic (growing on living organic matter) and within each morphological series a line of advance towards parasitism is usually evident. Although the overall evolutionary trend is from simple to complex structures, many of the highly evolved terrestrial fungi have some structures which are simple, or lack some structures, owing to later degeneration. Such a reversal of the general trend tends to obscure relationships.

The very small size of bacteria and the simplicity of their fine structure set them apart from the fungi which are far larger organisms with a predominantly filamentous form, or even a massive plant body, and cell structure similar to that of other simple plants. The viruses, known only as disease agents, are particles much smaller than bacteria. They have no independent life but grow only inside the cells of suitable organisms. They might be thought to lie between the living and non-living state except that their growth is based on an already organized living cell which they parasitize, and independently they have no metabolism.

Under natural conditions fungi and bacteria live in integrated communities and complex environments subject to constant change. Soil is a great reservoir of these organisms, which survive and grow in it prolifically. Most of our knowledge of them has been derived from pure cultures, in which one species is isolated by special techniques and then grown alone in various sterilized media where it can be seen clearly and its behaviour observed. The study of fungi and bacteria is essentially experimental. The small size of individual colonies, their rapid expansion in culture and, for most of them, their independence of light make them relatively easy to handle. In a laboratory a very large number of artificial habitats with carefully controlled conditions can be prepared for them and their reactions to all kinds of changes and many different nutrients quickly determined.

Bacterial cells have an average diameter of about $1\,\mu$ (1 micron $= 0.001$ mm) and that of many fungal hyphae and spores is about $10\,\mu$, which is small compared with the dimension of green plant cells which are often $20–50\,\mu$ or more in diameter. However, the main difference between these micro-organisms and higher plants is not in individual cell size but in cell aggregation. Bacteria and some fungi always grow as unicells. Filamentous fungi grow as separate threads or hyphae which only exceptionally coalesce to form a 'body'. The small size of fungal spores and individual bacteria allows them to be dispersed almost everywhere. They contaminate all kinds of material and all places unless special precautions are taken to exclude them. Minute amounts of nutrients will support the growth of many individuals, and the rate of increase of organisms of these small dimensions is on a different scale from that of larger plants. A thousandfold increase in numbers or in total hyphal length may follow under moderately favourable conditions after 10–24 hours of growth, and optimum conditions allow more rapid growth still. Some higher plants may show as great an increase after a year's growth, but many progress much more slowly.

The high surface-to-volume ratio of bacteria and fungi allows a free exchange of materials with the surroundings, and so permits rapid rates of metabolism and growth. Translocation within such small structures is minimal, as they penetrate or make close contact with their food over a large part of their surface. Besides allowing rapid absorption of useful substances, the large exposed surface is also vulnerable to unfavourable external conditions or to toxins which have a rapid effect. Large organisms have the ability to produce favourable conditions for their cells within their bodies, but micro-organisms are always directly influenced by external conditions.

Small size allows organisms to be destroyed easily, but this hazard is offset by their rapid growth rate and usually prolific production of reproductive cells. The very wide distribution of micro-organisms and their penetration into materials and substrates also hinder total destruction of a population. Even when unfavourable conditions of some sort kill large numbers, a few are likely to survive in unaffected sites from which they can spread out again when favourable conditions return, and then their power of rapid reproduction may result in the speedy re-establishment of a large population.

Both bacteria and fungi are of such special economic importance that the sciences of bacteriology and mycology are well developed. Bacteria are perhaps best known as the germs causing disease, and in this respect are of such enormous importance that bacteriology is usually studied as a medical subject. It is probably true, however, that the beneficial bacteria, particularly those of the soil, are more important.

Loss of stored products due to attack by moulds is a serious problem which can reach catastrophic proportions in the warmth and humidity of the tropics. In agriculture and horticulture war is always being waged against diseases caused by fungi (blights, mildews, rusts, etc.) which reduce the value of economic crops and occasionally destroy them completely. Poisonous toadstools are a hazard for the unwary epicure. Many fungi, however, are beneficial. The numerous saprophytes which rapidly break down dead organic matter, particularly forest litter, are vital in converting waste material and returning it to the soil. One type of fungus, yeast, has ancient and venerable practical application in the production of bread and wine. Likewise choice edible toadstools have long been used to flavour food. A new development which has rapidly assumed great importance is the manufacture of antibiotics which are complex antagonistic substances produced by some micro-organisms in culture. In their natural environment these substances may help to retard the growth of competitors. Important uses are being found in medicine and agriculture for an increasing number of them.

PART I

CELL ORGANIZATION AND PHYSIOLOGY

I

Morphology and Development

CELL STRUCTURE AND DEVELOPMENT OF BACTERIA

Bacteria are exceedingly small, simple unicells, spherical, ovoid or rod-shaped, the rods being straight, curved or spiral. As the shape of these tiny organisms is their only readily visible character it is used as a basis for describing them. *Cocci* (sing. coccus) are simple spherical or ellipsoidal cells. Some tend to stick together in pairs, e.g. *Diplococcus* spp. Tetrads of cocci are formed by *Micrococcus* spp., and in *Sarcina* spp. the cells divide regularly in three planes to form packets with rows of cells. In *Streptococcus* spp. cells are attached in chains, and in *Staphylococcus* spp. they form grape-like clusters. There are many genera of more or less straight rods which are all termed **bacilli** (sing. bacillus). The curved rods include *Vibrio* spp. which appear comma shaped. Some long cork-screw-shaped rods are included in the genus *Spirillum* (Fig. 1.1).

The diameter of bacterial cells is generally about 1 μ, so that in round figures 1 mg of wet weight of cocci contains about 1,000 million cells. Yet, within a single cell which is much smaller than the nucleus of most plant cells, all the functions of an individual organism are carried out. Bacterial cells grow and reproduce themselves, often very rapidly. Little structural detail can be seen in such small bodies with an ordinary light microscope, even with special staining methods and careful use of phase-contrast. The electron microscope gives pictures of thin sections of organisms at magnifications from ten to a hundred times greater than anything possible by the older methods and consequently reveals details of fine structure quite unknown before these instruments were developed. With their aid a new study known as 'fine structure' has been developed and knowledge of cell detail has been greatly extended.

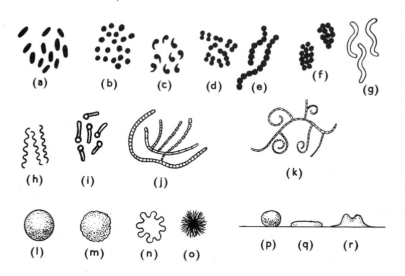

Fig. 1.1 Types of bacterial forms : (a) bacilli ; (b) cocci ; (c) comma vibrio ; (d) diplococci ; (e) streptococci ; (f) staphylococci ; (g) spirilla ; (h) spirochaetes ; (i) bacilli with endospores ; (j and k) *Streptomyces*. Types of bacterial colonies : (l) smooth ; (m) rough ; (n) lobed ; (o) spreading ; (p) raised ; (q) flat ; (r) raised with sunken centre. (Diagrams not to scale.)

Cell wall

Each bacterial cell is surrounded by a comparatively thick rigid wall, on the outside of which is a thin layer of slime. Under some conditions of growth this may become swollen to make a definite gelatinous sheath or capsule. Some bacteria may produce a mass of loose spreading slime which encloses colonies. The wall, which is inert and does not stain readily, is of complex composition which differs in different species. The main component is a mucopeptide substance composed of acetylglucosamine and acetylmuramic acid molecules linked alternately in a chain. Each acetylmuramic acid molecule carries a short peptide side chain containing alanine, glutamine and either lysine or diaminopimelic acid. Other compounds including proteins, polysaccharides and sometimes lipids may be present as an addition to this basic structure. Muramic acid is a compound always present and known only from the walls of bacteria. The compound di-aminopimelic acid which commonly occurs in bacterial walls and also in those of some blue-green algae (Cyanophyceae) appears to be absent from yeasts and moulds. Techoic acids are closely associated with the surface structures of many Gram-positive bacteria. Synthesis of both mucopeptide and ribitol techoic acids by intact *Staphylococcus aureus* is prevented by penicillin. It has been suggested that techoic acids in cells are connected with surface function or with biosynthesis of the cell envelope. The wall, which is shown by the electron microscope to have a granular structure, is permeable and allows solutions to reach the protoplasmic surface which it protects from such solid or colloidal particles as might pass through the slime. The enveloping layer of slime usually consists of complex poly-saccharides, characteristic of the species, or sometimes of polypeptides of high molecular weight, or sometimes of both together. For some pathogens of higher animals, production of a capsule prevents destruction of cells in the host tissues by white blood corpuscles and so favours progress of the disease. If the bacterial wall and its slime coating are removed by an enzyme capable of digesting wall material only, and the process is carried out in sufficiently strong sugar solution to prevent osmotic rupture, the naked protoplast rounds off, showing that the wall gives the cell its characteristic shape, and also allows it to maintain a much higher osmotic pressure than that of the solutions in which it normally lives.

Flagella (sing. flagellum)

These confer motility and may be present. They are fine filaments of uniform thickness, about 20 mμ (1 mμ = 0·001 μ). Each appears to consist of two or three protein molecules twisted tightly together. In electron micrographs flagella may be seen as rope-like structures coiled in an open wave form, each arising from a cytoplasmic granule. Analysis of flagella has shown them to consist entirely of a protein called 'flagellin' which is similar to myosin of contractile muscle fibres. Flagella on an individual bacterium are seldom single but are usually fairly numerous, and may be *polar*, arising at one or both ends of the cell, or *peritrichous*, arising all over the surface (Fig. 1.2).

Fimbriae (sing. fimbria)

These are present on some bacteria as filaments about half as thick as flagella, shorter, and much more numerous. They do not appear to be concerned with locomotion, but may attach the bacteria to other cells such as the red blood corpuscles, and also may assist pellicle formation on the surface of liquid cultures. Those species able to produce fimbriae readily vary between a fimbriate stage in liquid media and a mainly non-fimbriate form on solid media.

The cytoplasmic membrane or plasmalemma

This is the outer surface of the protoplast and lies close inside the wall. This lipoprotein layer stains readily. It functions as the semi-permeable membrane controlling passage of dissolved substances in and out of the cell. In general these are transported across the membrane only when active metabolism is going on in the protoplasm. The *cytoplasm*, which is seen to be rather dense and highly refringent when viewed by a light

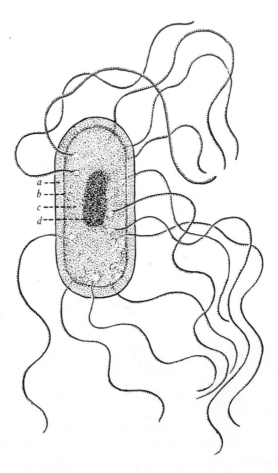

Fig. 1.2 Diagram of bacterial cell structure : (a) rigid wall ; (b) cytoplasmic membrane ; (c) cytoplasm with little structure ; (d) nuclear body. A number of peritrichous flagella are shown, each arising from a cytoplasmic granule (× c. 25,700).

microscope, is shown by electron micrography to contain numerous *ribosomes* which are minute bodies 10–30 mμ in diameter composed of ribonucleic acid (RNA) and protein. No other fine structure has been seen in the cytoplasm. Vacuoles are not present. Under certain conditions of growth there may be a few storage granules of volutin, polysaccharide including glycogen, lipid globules or protein crystals. Mitochondria (p.13) are absent and in bacterial cytoplasm there is little evidence of a localization of metabolic reactions such as that recognized in cytoplasm of higher plant cells, though in some cases particles of bacterial cytoplasmic membrane have shown respiratory activity.

Nuclear material

Since electron micrographs have been available a definite nuclear apparatus has been recognized though it differs from the much larger, highly organized nucleus of normal plant and animal cells. In bacteria it is spherical to ovoid in resting cells, elongated or dumb-bell-shaped in dividing cells, but always lacks a nuclear membrane. A single ring-shaped chromosome appears to be the usual form, and this has been seen in electron micrographs in process of duplication in cells preparing to divide. This ring stains with Feulgen reagent which reacts specifically with deoxyribonucleic acid (DNA), the characteristic gene substance.

Endospores

Some species of bacteria, mainly those of the genera *Clostridium* and *Bacillus* are able to form extremely resistant endospores, either from the central part of the cell or from one or both ends. From one-quarter to one half of the cell volume is enclosed in an ovoid spore envelope forming a highly refractive body impervious to ordinary stains. This structure is very resistant to high and low temperatures, and to disinfectants, and may survive for many years. In some species of *Azotobacter* the entire cell forms a similar resistant structure which is then called a *cyst*.

Cultivation

Before a species of bacterium can be recognized and examined it must be isolated from its surroundings. When this has been accomplished, usually by dilution techniques and use of selective media, a *pure culture* of the single species can be grown. Laboratory methods are explained in detail in such handbooks as *Bacteriology Illustrated* by Gillies and Dodds (p. 185). Pure cultures may be maintained in various aqueous solutions or on the same media solidified as a gel with agar, gelatine or hydrated silica, and then the individual appearance and behaviour of the species can be determined (Fig. 1.1, l–r). For preliminary examination with a microscope and for testing stain reactions a **smear** is prepared by spreading a drop from a culture on the centre of a slide and drying this gently over a Bunsen flame. The slime layer cements the dried cells to the slide which can then be stained by pouring alcoholic or aqueous dyes directly on the dried material. The excess stain may be washed off with alcohol or acetone. The resulting preparation shows that the cells have approximately the same shape, size and general appearance as living cells mounted in aqueous solution. No other living cells can be treated in this manner without destroying their structure, which shows that the minute bacterium is very different from other kinds of living cells.

Staining properties

The staining properties of dried and fixed bacterial cells are of special importance in identification because they depend on the chemical, and thus the physiological, properties of the cytoplasm and cell membrane of organisms which may differ widely in these respects yet have the same morphological characters. The Gram staining procedure is by far the most useful and important one in bacteriology. **Gram-positive** organisms when treated with a para-rosaniline dye, such as crystal violet, and subsequently with iodine, form a stain complex which is fixed in the cell from which it is not removed by the ordinary decolorizing agents, alcohol or acetone. **Gram-negative** organisms treated in the same way are rendered colourless and may thus be stained with a contrasting dye such as neutral red which makes them appear red in contrast to the violet Gram-positive cells. The cell wall of Gram-positive organisms consists mainly of the mucopeptide base with only traces of lipids, and only a few of the possible amino acids. Gram-negative walls in contrast contain considerable additional substances with up to 20 per cent lipid and a wide range of amino acids. The second most generally used stain test is for ability to hold a dye under acid conditions. Organisms are described as **acid-fast** if they retain a dye with which they have been heated, when they are subsequently washed with acid-alcohol. If the organisms are not acid-fast they are decolorized by the acid-alcohol treatment. Acid-fast organisms have been shown to contain extra lipids and the acid-fast character is thought to be due to the special nature of the cell membrane.

Bacterial colonies

On solid media inoculated with dispersed bacteria small colonies visible to the naked eye are soon formed. The colony of each species has constant characters which are of assistance in identification: the points to note are colour, form and shape (raised, flat or in a film), surface (smooth, matt, glistening, rough), and margin (lobed, spreading or entire) (Fig. 1.1).

Development of different forms of bacteria

The maximum cell size of any species is fairly constant, and when colonies of bacteria are growing freely cells divide when they reach this maximum. First the chromatinic body divides and then the protoplast cleaves in two with formation of a double transverse membrane. A new dividing wall grows inwards as a ring from the margin and meets in the centre; finally this crosswall splits transversely into two walls so that two complete separate daughter cells are formed, each half the maximum size. Under favourable conditions this process of simple division or *binary fission* may proceed rapidly (up to one division each 20 minutes) so that large populations of very similar cells result. For certain rod-shaped species, growth of the cell appears to occur mainly at one end which is cut off when the cell divides. This modified fission approaches a budding form of growth.

Usually cell division is a very exact process resulting in identical daughter cells, so that bacteria breed true and maintain constant characters from generation to generation. Occasionally, however, some of the progeny vary. In culture such very large numbers of individuals and generations arise in such a short period that variations are fairly frequently encountered. Some of these are non-heritable variations; most, however, are heritable mutations.

Adaptation

On certain media some colonies may undergo adaptive changes, such as being able to grow on a nutrient which they were previously unable to utilize. Such a change may be due to the formation of adaptive enzymes which are formed by the bacterial cells only when the substrate on which they act is present. When the cells are first placed in contact with this medium they are unable to act on it till the necessary enzyme has been synthesized in sufficient quantity. Such variation is obviously a response to the environment and is readily reversible by reversing the conditions which induced it.

Mutation

Bacterial cells contain probably over 1,000 genes, each corresponding with a specific segment of a DNA molecule. Duplication of genes must precede cell division. If anything affects or alters a gene at any stage a sudden, heritable change, known as a mutation, occurs. In bacterial populations mutations are frequent and obvious. The effect of an altered gene does not appear to be masked by an unmutated partner gene; thus it is suggested that bacterial cells are haploid, having only one set of genes and not a diploid set.

Mutations arise spontaneously in bacteria just as they do in other organisms, and also they may be promoted, or their rate of production increased, by treatment with X-rays and other high-energy radiation, or with certain chemical compounds. Mutations involving cell structure have not been found, but some affecting the appearance of colonies, such as the change from rough to smooth, are well known. The most interesting and the most important which have been examined are the many physiological mutations which involve a change in the ability of the cell to produce or to utilize some compound. New strains or **mutants** with limited synthetic ability have often been important research tools in studying biochemical reactions.

Pleomorphism and involution

Pleomorphism, the possession of more than one form or shape of cell, and involution, meaning the formation of abnormal cell shapes, may occur in the course of growth, particularly in ageing cultures growing on artificial media or in some species under acid conditions. In the presence of drugs or antibiotics, abnormal cell forms may be produced often differing grossly from the normal. They may be swollen or of irregular shape, e.g. pear-shaped or in filaments with irregular thickenings. Many are non-viable but some revert to the original form when transferred to a suitable fresh medium. In some cases these degenerate cells appear to be the result of defective wall synthesis. It is known that the antibiotic penicillin exerts its bactericidal action by interfering with cell wall formation, resulting in non-viable cells lacking walls.

Large bodies and L-forms

Under certain conditions of shock such as unfavourable temperature or drug treatment, many bacteria produce very large fragile cells called 'large bodies' which lack a cell wall. If normal conditions are restored fairly quickly the bacteria may recover and grow and divide normally. If the unfavourable conditions continue the cells either die or become stabilized as L-forms, which consist of minute filterable cells together with large globules of cytoplasm devoid of walls, a condition which is like the normal growth form of the pleuro-pneumonia organisms. They may grow and re-produce in this form for many generations, but they frequently revert to the bacterial form of the strain from which they were derived. They are extreme-ly resistant to penicillin even when the parent strain in its normal form is very susceptible. Some authorities regard them as laboratory artifacts.

Gonidia

A number of bacteria produce minute flagellate cells named 'gonidia' about which very little is yet known.

Life cycles

As for other types of micro-organisms the life cycles involve a regular succession of different types of cells. Although the various cell forms described above are now well established for certain bacterial species and strains, it is not known whether they are produced in any particular cycle.

Sexuality in bacteria

Combination of hereditary characters has been demonstrated for the species *Escherichia coli*. Two strains with different nutritional requirements were mixed together for a short period, then cells were isolated from the progeny and re-examined. It was found that a large proportion showed combination of the parental characters. Electron micrographs have been obtained of *cell fusion* by means of a cytoplasmic bridge which would allow exchange or transfer of genetic material, and thus produce such a combination of hereditary characters. Two other methods of recombination of characters in bacteria are known. Bacterial cells may undergo *transformation* by absorption of a 'transforming principle' from a filtrate of another strain of the organism. This principle has been isolated and analysed and shown to consist of DNA. Pure DNA may also be removed from bacterial cells by particles of virus nature known as bacteriophage, or simply 'phage' (p. 22), which can carry it and implant it in other cells. This process, which also results in genetic change in the organism, is named *transduction*. Thus if phage attacks a culture of mixed strains of organisms the survivors may show combinations of the characters present individually in the original strains.

STRUCTURE AND DEVELOPMENT OF FUNGI

The thallus

A very few simple fungi are unicellular, e.g. chytrids in the Chytridiomycetes and yeasts in the Ascomycetes. The single yeast cells grow by a special form of budding during which a small bulge formed on the parent cell enlarges till it is about quarter-sized, when the neck between it and the parent constricts and cuts it off. On solid media yeasts grow in colonies of separate cells similar to bacterial colonies. Most fungi, however, form long slender filaments called *hyphae*, which usually branch freely and intertwine to form a flocculent mass named the *mycelium*. In the lower fungi the hyphae are mostly without septa and form long, much-branched coenocytic cells. The cylindrical walls are lined with living cytoplasm containing many small nuclei. Young hyphae are completely filled with protoplasm, but there are large vacuoles in older parts of the mycelium, while the oldest parts may become emptied and cut off with crosswalls.

In the higher fungi (Ascomycetes and Basidiomycetes) the hyphae are divided by frequent septa which may cut off regular, small, cell-like divisions, or more usually make long cylindrical segments. The septa are not formed as a result of nuclear division but grow inwards from a ring on the hyphal wall, and do not necessarily cut off uni- or bi-nucleate fragments. A pore remains open at the centre of each crosswall through which cytoplasm may stream, and through which nuclei have been seen to pass, though in older septa the openings may become blocked. In Ascomycetes and some Fungi Imperfecti the pore is a simple hole in the middle of a transverse wall which is thicker at the outside margin (Plate 3A). In Basidiomycetes the pore is a complex structure named a dolipore, which has been shown by electron micrography to be surrounded by a thickened rim, and to be protected above and below by caplike covers. These appear in section as brackets and so are called parenthesomes (Plate 3B). Under some conditions they may close the passage. Hyphae may become thickwalled especially in parts of fungal fruiting bodies and the walls may be variously ornamented. Parasitic fungi may form small hyphal pegs which penetrate the epidermis of the plants on which they grow thus opening the internal tissues to attack. The victim from which the parasite draws food is named the *host*. The highly specialized parasites, known as *obligate parasites*, which can grow only on other living organisms, characteristically form *haustoria* (sing. haustorium) which are modified absorbing hyphae pushed into the host's living cells which they manage to rob without killing. Some endotrophic mycorrhizal fungi (p. 87) form similar structures which the host cells appear to be able to use by absorbing their contents, turning the tables, as it were, on a potential parasite.

In Ascomycetes and Basidiomycetes hyphae have a tendency to anastomose and may form a woven mass called *plectenchyma*. Where this consists obviously of long hyphae woven and fused it is called *prosenchyma*, but where it is formed from hyphae with small regular divisions, so presenting a cellular appearance, it is called *pseudo-parenchyma*. The higher Ascomycetes and Basidiomycetes may form large fruiting bodies, or *sporophores*, composed of these 'tissues'. There is great diversity among these large structures as to form, texture and colour. Some formed rapidly in a favourable season are ephemeral growths which carry and aid dispersal of the sexually produced spores. Some woody bracket fungi reach a metre in diameter, and are solid enough to last for years, but these are exceptions.

Many fungi also form somewhat indefinite solid bodies called *stromata* (sing. stroma) from plectenchyma of either type. Reproductive structures or fructifications commonly develop in or from such bodies (Fig. 3.5). Some species produce *sclerotia* which are tough, resting bodies, formed usually of pseudo-parenchyma in which the outer cells are thick-walled and the inner are stocked with food. They are able to survive unfavourable periods or seasons after which they may germinate to form a mycelial growth, or they may give rise to fructifications. Some hyphae may grow fused together in string-like strands with a tough outside cover. These root-like structures called **rhizomorphs** may creep under bark of trees, or underground, and serve to spread a fungus from one favourable place across alien territory to another source of suitable food. The well-known damaging tree parasite *Armillaria mellea*, the honey or boot-lace fungus, spreads from one victim to the next in this way. The diversity of thallus form in various groups of fungi is described in some of the later chapters.

The hyphal wall

This is built of layers of polysaccharide, the macromolecules of which are either in the form of long, more or less straight chains, or of branched chains. The straight-chain polymers are laid down in parallel bundles forming microfibrils. Ideally walls are built up in two or three layers in each of which the fibrils are more or less parallel, but in the successive layers the lines of fibrils cross, building a strong yet extensible lattice. In one group of Oomycetes the fibrous skeleton of the wall consists mainly of cellulose, in some species with a lipid surface, but in most fungi it is made largely of chitin mixed with cellulose or other polymers. Cellulose is a more or less straight-chain glucopyranose polymer of 500 or more units. Chitin consists of similar chains of acetylglucosamine. Other polysaccharides which have been found in hyphal walls are mannan, a branched-chain polymer of mannose, and glucan, a branched-chain polymer of glucopyranose (Fig. 1.3). Associated or mixed with these pure compounds there may be heteropolysaccharides, the macromolecules of which contain different units. Amyloid compounds which stain blue with iodine occur regularly in some hyphal walls, especially in fruiting bodies of members of certain families and genera of higher fungi. The walls of some fungal cells, e.g. some sporangia, are thickened, complex and may be studded with crystals, and walls of spores are often complex.

The wall is thinner at the tips of the hyphae than in the older parts. The actual end dome of the hyphal wall appears to be rigid and perhaps protective as it pushes forward. Extension occurs in the adjacent part of the lateral wall which remains soft and elastic, and it is here that branches begin as buds pushed out from the parent hypha which, later, is cut off by a dividing wall (Fig. 1.4).

Flagella

These occur on the motile cells formed by Chytridiomycetes and Oomycetes such as zoospores and motile gametes, which are protoplasts enclosed within a cytoplasmic membrane, but without a cell wall. Fungal flagella are larger and more complex than those of the bacteria. Each flagellum is made of 11 distinct, parallel filaments, 2 of which are centrally placed, the remainder being peripheral. They arise in a bundle from a cytoplasmic body called the **blepharoplast** which is attached by a strand to the nucleus. There are two types of flagella, **whiplash** and **tinsel** (Plate 1). The first has a rigid base formed of all 11 strands from which the central pair are extended to form the end lash. The tinsel flagella are

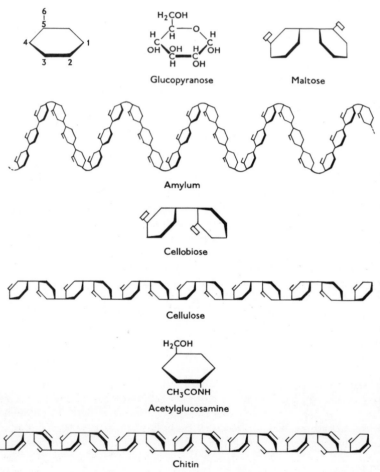

Glucopyranose

Maltose

Amylum

Cellobiose

Cellulose

Acetylglucosamine

Chitin

Fig. 1.3 Diagram of structure of some polysaccharide molecules.

covered with a delicate fur of short slender threads. The whiplash flagellar structure is found in other motile cells as diverse as the antherozoids of mosses or the spermatozoa of mammals, and so is of great interest and biological importance. Very clear electron micrographs of the flagella of zoospores of *Phytophthora erythroseptica* have shown additional exceedingly fine hair-like endings to the fibres covering the tinsel flagellum and similar very fine extensions from the thicker part of the whiplash flagellum (Plate 1).

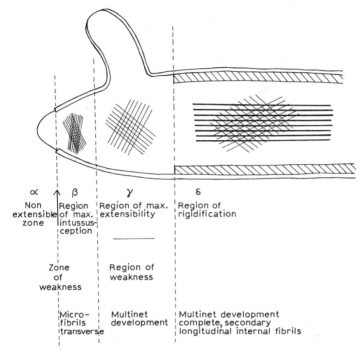

Fig. 1.4 Diagram illustrating the organization of the hyphal apex. (From Burnett, J. H., 1968, *Fundamentals of Mycology*, Arnold, London.)

Cytoplasm

The fine structure of cytoplasm has as yet been examined in only a few fungi. **Endoplasmic reticulum**, which is seen plainly in electron micrographs of higher plant cells where it appears as an organized system of membranes bounding ultra-minute canals, is not usually as well developed in fungal cytoplasm. **Ribosomes** have been demonstated in the cytoplasm of some fungi as they have been in bacteria. In higher plant cells ribosomes which are mostly seated on the endoplasmic reticulum have been identified as the centres of protein synthesis. **Mitochondria**, small, oval, cytoplasmic organelles about 1 μ long, are well developed and have a structure essentially similar to that of the comparable bodies in other cells. They are bounded by a double membrane and have internal parallel plates named *cristae* also formed of lipid-protein membranes. They are the sites of the different respiratory enzyme reactions and of synthesis of adenosine tri-phosphate (ATP). Cytoplasmic vesicles which appear to be bounded by membranes may be seen arising in the cytoplasm of rapidly elongating hyphae where, it has been suggested, they collapse to form endoplasmic reticulum. Stored food may be present as granules of glycogen, which is an α-glucopyranose polymer like starch or, often, as droplets of fat. Vacuoles also may contain glycogen or other reserve food (Plates 2 and 3A and B).

Nuclei

In the peripheral cytoplasm of older vegetative hyphae the nuclei are small, or very small, but in some reproductive cells they are large and conspicuous. They stain in the usual way with Feulgen reagent and are seen to be organized like the nuclei of higher plants. Chromosomes have been seen in dividing nuclei and counted in some species, though details of nuclear division are not always exactly similar to those in higher plants. In most fungi the nuclei are haploid except immediately after a sexual fusion when a diploid nucleus is formed in the zygote, this condition reverting to the haploid at the first division, when meiosis occurs. Recently cytological studies of some Oomycetes have shown that they may be diploid in the vegetative phase.

Spores

The common propagative units of fungi are spores, which may be pro-duced sexually or asexually, and which are usually small simple unicells, or less frequently consist of 2 or more cells. The multiplicity and variety of spore production and its prolific scale is one of the chief characters of fungi which are thus able to reproduce themselves so readily under so many different conditions that they can exploit all the available suitable sub-strata. The spores may have a foodstore in the form of oil drops and normally contain dense cytoplasm. Many are short-lived, and if they fail to reach a place favourable to growth they soon die. The majority of spores are air-borne, often after being actively shot off, or out, into the air. Their size, shape, colour, ornamentation, chemical reaction and the manner of production are all constantly characteristic of the species (Fig. 4.5). Since thallus characters are similar for large groups of fungi, spore characters are useful in defining and diagnosing individual species. The walls of many spores are complex, with up to three distinct layers having different stain-ing properties. The outermost layer is often pigmented and/or sculptured (Plate 3C and D). Amyloid compounds which stain dark blue with iodine are characteristic of spore walls of fungi of some groups.

Sexual reproduction

In fungi as in other organisms sexual reproduction involves fusion of two nuclei to form a zygote nucleus. Sex organs where present are called *gametangia.* In the simplest examples of sexual reproduction in fungi similar motile gametes from equal gametangia fuse together in pairs as they do in the sexual reproduction of many simple algae, but as similar motile cells behave as zoospores, sexual reproduction in these simple types is not as distinctly organized as it is in higher forms. Many of the fungi which develop sex organs have small male gametangia and larger female gametangia. The male, called *antheridia* (sing. antheridium), fuse with the female organs, which are called *oogonia* (sing. oogonium) if they contain large egg cells. Gametangial contents mix before the sexual fusion of the nuclei takes place. In one small aquatic group, the Monoblepharidales, motile antherozoids are produced in the antheridia. They are shed into the water and swim to the oogonia in each of which is a single sessile egg cell. In the well-known group of terrestrial fungi, the Zygomycetes, the gametangia and their contents which fuse together are more or less equal in size. In this group the fused gametangia which contain a number of zygotes develop into a thick-walled zygospore.

In the higher Ascomycetes, and especially in the Basidiomycetes, the equivalent of the diploid phase is developed in a unique manner, in *dikaryotic* cells or mycelium. After sexual fusion of cells and mingling of the cytoplasm, a stage called plasmogamy, the nuclei which represent two gametes become paired and lie side by side. They persist and multiply for a longer or shorter period in pairs or *dikaryons.* As the hyphae or mycelial cells which contain them grow, these paired nuclei divide simultaneously producing further pairs. Finally the dikaryon fuses together in the young ascus or basidium to form a zygote nucleus which immediately undergoes meiosis and haploid spores are formed.

In some Ascomycetes pairing occurs after fusion of two gametangia, or after fertilization of the large multinucleate, female gametangium, the *ascogonium*, by small, non-motile male cells, called *spermatia*, which are shed from other mycelia and carried by air currents or even insects; or ascogonia may be fertilized by conidia. In other Ascomycetes, however, no sex organs are formed and pairing of nuclei follows fusion of the cytoplasm of vegetative cells. After such fusions a group of dikaryotic cells or ascogenous hyphae develops within the young fructification. Fusion of nuclei takes place finally in the special terminal cells called *asci* (sing. ascus), and this is always followed immediately by meiosis and formation in the ascus of the haploid ascospores, each of which may germinate to grow into a new haploid mycelium.

In the Basidiomycetes the dikaryotic stage is prolonged and, in the more advanced members of this group, forms a long-lived mycelium which may be the main phase of the organism. Fusion of nuclei, followed by meiosis, takes place in the special terminal cells called *basidia* (sing. basidium), before the formation of the haploid basidiospores each of which may

germinate to give a haploid mycelium consisting of uninucleate cells
(Fig. 1.5a). In the rust fungi the dikaryotic stage is brought about by fertilization of one haploid mycelium by spermatia produced by another
haploid mycelium, but other Basidiomycetes lack any kind of sex cells or
sex organs. Dikaryotomy, the condition with paired nuclei or dikaryons,
follows fusion between cells or hyphae of two vegetative haploid mycelia.
When a suitable nucleus from one haploid mycelium passes into another it
may divide rapidly, and the daughter nuclei migrate quickly throughout
the haploid mycelium, forming dikaryons in all cells in a short space of time.

As the dikaryotic mycelium grows it normally forms conspicuous *clamp
connections* which can be taken as a sign of dikaryotic growth. Before the
paired nuclei divide, the hyphal end containing them forms a large bulge

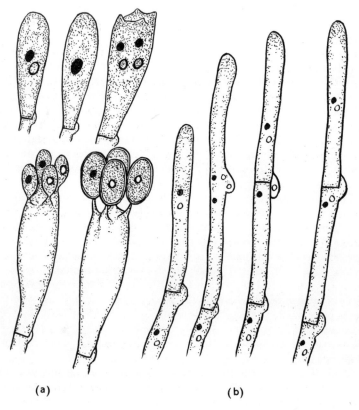

(a)   (b)

Fig. 1.5 Diagrams illustrating : (a) stages in development of a basidium with 4
basidiospores ; (b) stages in formation of a clamp connection.

or short side branch which accommodates one of the dividing nuclei, whilst the other divides in the main hypha. One daughter nucleus from each member of the pair migrates into the elongating tip and forms a new dikaryon, and a septum formed behind them cuts off the base of the hypha with one daughter nucleus, and also the short branch containing the other. The short branch then clamps on to the basal hypha and the walls between them dissolve so that the other pair of nuclei can move together to form a dikaryon in the sub-apical cell of the hypha (Fig. 1.5b). Although these clamp connections are typical of dikaryotic mycelium and are seen in the majority of Basidiomycete fructifications, many Basidiomycetes and almost all other fungi lack them. Exceptionally wide hyphae in parts of a fungal mycelium which normally forms clamps may grow without them.

Asexual reproduction

Most fungi produce both sexual and asexual spores. Except for the higher Basidiomycetes asexual reproduction is generally more important for spreading the species because more asexual spores are formed. There may be more than one kind of them, and they may be formed over a long period, or even more or less continuously during growth. In fact for several thousand known species of fungi asexual reproduction is so common that sexual reproduction has either become very infrequent and is seldom seen, or else it has been suppressed and is never found at all. In the latter case the species are classified in the Fungi Imperfecti on the basis of their asexual stages only, although by comparison with asexual stages of fungi which are known to produce sexual spores, it is clear that most are Ascomycetes which have lost the ability to form asci.

Various types of asexual spores may be formed. Some fungi, particularly when cultured in a sugary medium, grow in the form of regularly divided hyphae in which all the cells round off and separate into a mass of **oidia**. These resemble the buds produced by yeast, and in fact in some cases oidia may develop into a yeast-like growth. In some fungi certain cells in the hyphae may become thick-walled, resting **chlamydospores** which are capable of outliving the parent mycelium. Asexual spores in the lower fungi are mostly produced in special enlarged cells called sporangia, the contents of which separate to form a larger or smaller number of **sporangiospores**. In water moulds and some other fungi of damp habitats these are flagellated zoospores, but in forms like *Rhizopus* each sporangium liberates a large number of small, air-borne spores.

In some advanced Oomycetes each sporangium is a small cell which is shed and which germinates like a single spore. *Phytophthora infestans*, the potato blight fungus, and some related species are of special interest in this connection because the small, single-celled sporangia which they shed may either germinate directly into new hyphae or, if conditions are suitable, they may liberate internally-formed zoospores. In other fungi and particularly in the Ascomycetes, asexual spores called *conidia* are produced on special aerial hyphae, usually budded successively in chains from special cells called *phialides*, and are often produced in enormous numbers.

MYXOMYCETES OR MYCETOZOA (SLIME MOULDS)

The list of possible alternative names for this group is an indication that they are a separate class of uncertain affinity. The majority of these organisms produce pigmented spores in small, delicate sporangia, which are at most a few millimetres tall and which are often studded with tiny crystals of a calcium salt. The small, spherical spores, which are often mixed with a capillitium of fine threads, are characteristic of each species and are surrounded by a two-layered wall which may be sculptured or spiny on the outside. The exact composition of the wall remains uncertain.

Plasmodium formation

When the spore germinates the wall bursts and the protoplasmic contents emerge and form 1–4 biflagellate swarm cells, or zoospores, which swim in surface moisture. These may divide and reproduce themselves, or they may form amoeboid cells known as *myxamoebae*, which also reproduce by division or revert to swarm cells. All these unicells may feed saprophytically or by ingesting solid particles of organic food. At some stage the cells fuse in pairs to form zygotes which may then divide repeatedly. At length many of these cells formed after the sexual fusion coalesce to form a large, multinucleate, amoeboid mass of protoplasm called the *plasmodium* (Fig. 1.6). This animal-like thallus which is in the form of a network or sheet of granular protoplasm, with many small nuclei and numerous small vacuoles, creeps over rotten wood or soil, or under flakes of bark, avoiding light and feeding on microscopic organisms or fragments of organic matter which it ingests. The protoplasm circulates actively within this structure often flowing first in one direction and then streaming in reverse.

Under drought or cold the plasmodium may divide to form many plurinucleate cysts, or the whole plasmodium may dry to form a 'sclerotium' (which is not the same as a fungal sclerotium). These dried forms can germinate again, even after several years, to re-form a plasmodium. Under certain conditions, still not clearly understood, the plasmodium forms sporangia and spores, often creeping to a drier place in the open before doing so. At many points over the surface some of the protoplasm flows upwards, often with a pulsating movement. Finally clusters of slender

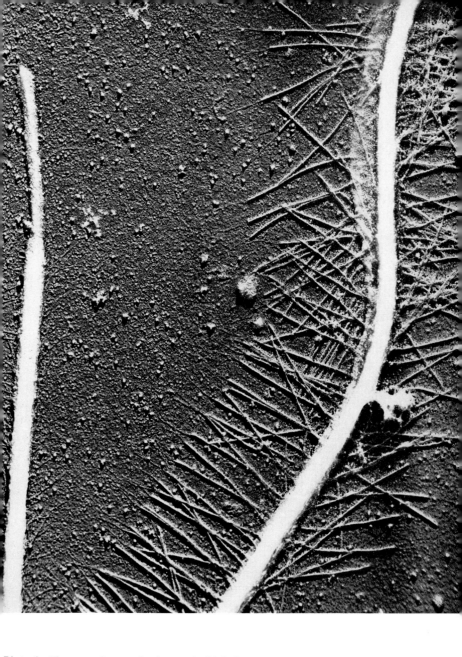

Plate 1 Electron micrograph of part of whiplash and tinsel flagella of zoospore of *Phytophthora erythroseptica* showing hairs on the whiplash flagellum and fine terminal portions of hairs on the tinsel flagellum. ×9,100. (From Vujicuc, R., Colhoun, J. and Chapman, J. A., *Trans. Br. mycol. Soc.*, **51**, 127, Pl. 7.)

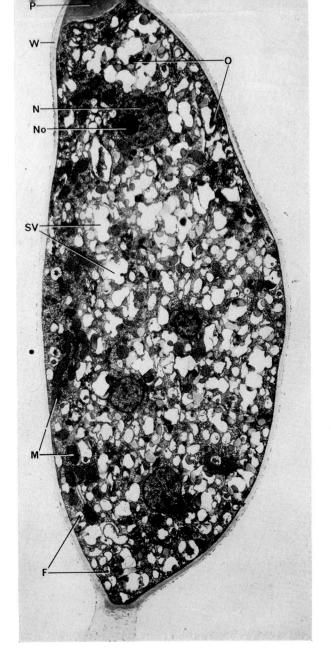

Plate 2 Electron micrograph of median longitudinal section of a young, unchilled sporangium of *Phytophthora infestans* illustrating the random distribution of storage vesicles, (SV), mitochondria (M), osmiophilic inclusions (O), and flagella (F). The section includes four nuclei (N), one of which exhibits a nucleolus (No). The protoplasm is contained within a single-layered wall (W), which is pierced by an apical pore, plugged by the papilla (P). ×4,850. (From King, J. E., Colhoun, J. and Butler, R. D., *Trans. Br. mycol. Soc.* **51**, 280, Pl. 14.)

stalks and swollen sporangia are formed. A sterile columella and capillitium threads may develop with the spores inside the sporangial wall (Fig. 1.6). Before the spores are formed a meiotic division takes place and haploid, uninucleate spores develop.

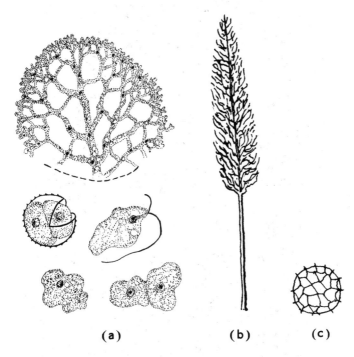

(a)   **(b)**   **(c)**

Fig. 1.6 (a) Part of a plasmodium net (×50) : (below) germinating spore, swarm cell, amoeboid cell (two cells fusing) (×1,000). (b) *Stemonitis fusca* sporangium with persistent columella and capillitium (×5). (c) *S. fusca* spore (×1,000).

A number of similar, though possibly not closely related organisms, are placed in this curious group which has some affinities with Protozoa and some with Fungi. The different forms which occur quite commonly are of considerable interest and much remains to be learned about them.

PLASMODIOPHORALES

A number of parasitic species belong to this order but the best known is *Plasmodiophora brassicae* which causes clubroot of species of *Brassica*.

The swarm cells are biflagellate with one long and one very short flagellum, both being of the whiplash type. The order does not appear to be closely related to other groups and has suffered considerable classificatory shuffling. Details of the life cycle are not known for certain though it is possible that gametes are formed and sexual fusion occurs. Plants are infected when zoospores in the soil enter root hairs. Within the root a mass of multinucleate protoplasm, a plasmodium, is formed, and root cells are stimulated to divide and form a clubroot which houses the parasite. The plasmodium divides to form a large number of resting spores which are shed into the soil when the clubroot is broken or decays. On germination each produces a zoospore.

ACRASIALES OR CELLULAR SLIME MOULDS

This is a group of organisms the members of which are abundant and widespread in soil. Like the true slime moulds they are a group the relationships of which are obscure. They can be cultured, together with soil bacteria on which they feed, in media made from hay infusions or leaf mould. They produce spores each of which may germinate to release a single amoeboid cell which feeds by engulfing bacteria. When the amoebae have multiplied to form a large population many of them aggregate round specific centres to form pseudo-plasmodia. Each cell retains its individuality but the tiny slug-like mass behaves as a unit. This may stream up or out to form a *sorocarp*, about 1 mm in height. In some examples this has a slender stalk of a cellulose cylinder within which the amoebae stream, and a globose cluster of walled spores at its head. Although this group of organisms has been studied by mycologists, some botanists think that its affinities are mainly with the Protozoa. The walled spores are not an animal character but they are formed in a manner different from fungal spores.

VIRUSES

These are the agents of a number of important and usually highly-infectious diseases of bacteria, plants, and animals, including man. Details of their structure have been worked out comparatively recently by combining the results of electron micrography and chemical analysis. Virus particles capable of infecting specific hosts range in size from a quarter to a tenth of that of the smallest bacteria down to some which are of the dimensions of large protein molecules. Because of their small size they pass through filters which remove bacteria from which they are thus easily separated: hence the term filtrable viruses. They can, however, be retained by finer filters now available. Filtrates containing viruses are highly infectious but none will produce growths in any of the media in which many bacteria normally grow readily. Characteristically virus infections are highly specific but a few viruses are known to attack more than one host.

Structure

Each virus particle or *virion* consists typically of a nucleic acid core covered by a tightly fitting protective coat, or *capsid*, of identical sub-units, or *capsomeres*, made up of molecules of one kind of protein, with a few molecules only of enzyme proteins. The nucleic acid is either ribonucleic acid, RNA, or deoxyribonucleic acid, DNA. Plant viruses contain RNA, the vast majority of bacterial viruses (*bacteriophages* or simply phages) contain DNA, while about half of the animal viruses contain DNA and half RNA. The proportion of nucleic acid varies from about 1–40 per cent. The composition of the larger viruses of animals is more complex as the virion may be contained in its own membrane; the influenza viruses contain in addition to RNA and coat protein about 5 per cent of polysaccharide, about 10 per cent of phospholipids, and 5 per cent cholesterol. Such lipid-containing viruses are sensitive to organic solvents, to bile salts, and to other surface-active agents. The pox group of viruses are even more complex. Vaccinia virus has a number of enzymes and co-enzymes as well as lipids all contained within a protective membrane. Even such large and complex virions, however, have no normal metabolic activity when freed from the host cells.

Bacteriophages have a special structure which may be associated with the need to penetrate the resistant bacterial cell wall. Each phage particle has a head which is spherical, ellipsoid, or hexagonal in outline, and a conspicuous tail (Plate 4A). In the T-even type of phages which attack *Escherichia coli* the tail has a basal plate carrying long slender threads which appear to anchor the virion to the wall of any susceptible cell which they may chance to touch. The tail, which then shortens by coiling, makes a hole in the wall through which the DNA migrates into the bacterium leaving the protein shell stuck on the outside. This protein component has been described as a 'disposable microsyringe' which injects the DNA.

All the viruses, even the simplest, appear to contain a few enzyme molecules which are primarily DNA or RNA polymerase with two components, firstly an enzyme which promotes the phosphodiester links which lead to the long chain of the molecule, and secondly an enzyme which promotes the base-pairing or copying which results in each new chain being an exact replica of its parent.

The protein shell or capsid of the virion is formed of identical molecules arranged in a geometrical pattern resulting in cubic, helical, or complex symmetry. The nucleic acid is usually single-stranded and may be in a long helix or in a coiled coil forming a ball. Both nucleic acid and protein are characteristic for each kind of virus but only the nucleic acid carries the infection. When virions are introduced into a susceptible cell they disorganize its metabolism resulting in replication of virus compounds instead of host cell material. The nucleic acid is formed in the nucleus while the virus protein is synthesized in the host cytoplasm. When new virus nucleic acid passes out of the nucleus its protein coat assembles round it in the cytoplasm and as it passes out of the host cell additional surface components may be added. Newly formed virus then spreads to more host cells or even throughout an entire organism. Occasionally the virus may have little effect but often it results in serious disease or even death.

If the nucleic acid fraction is separated from the protein and inoculated into a susceptible cell some disease results though the infection is not as severe as that due to complete virions. Capsid material alone has no effect. Although coat protein has been shown by electron micrographs to remain outside phage-infected bacteria, normal infection may be the result of nucleic acid together with some enzymes entering the host cells.

The first virus to be isolated in a pure state, and one which has been the subject of intensive experimentation, is that causing mosaic disease in the tobacco plant (TMV) (Plate 5A) and which may also attack tomatoes. Pure preparations of TMV can be made by centrifuging juice from infected plants so as to remove both the larger and smaller particles, and digesting the separated virus material with proteolytic enzymes which remove adhering cell proteins. The protein of the virus coat is formed of such a tightly fitting layer of molecules that it is very resistant to enzyme action. Electron micrographs of such purified TMV have shown rod-shaped particles, 300×15 mμ, with a central coil known from analyses to be RNA inside a cylinder of protein. The two parts have been separated and identified, and after separation have been reconstituted. The protein by itself has no activity, but the RNA of TMV, like that of a number of other viruses, when tested alone has some infectivity, but much less than that of the original virus. Although complete particles are very resistant to decomposition both RNA and protein separately are attacked readily by enzymes, and, as the special enzyme ribonuclease is very common in cells, any solitary RNA is likely to be destroyed quickly. The RNA inside its protein envelope forms a stable and viable particle.

Examples of virus diseases (see also p. 95)

Many kinds of plants may be infected by viruses, which may cause a mottled yellowing of leaves called leaf mosaic, or leaves may become crinkled or dwarfed. These diseases usually have a stunting effect with consequent reduction in yield of economic crops. Occasionally in horticultural plants the effect of the virus is prized even though the plant may be weakened. Striped tulips are infected by a virus causing breaking of the flower colour, a bizarre effect which was formerly highly valued. Many horticultural plants with variegated leaves owe this special feature to a virus infection. Important human diseases caused by viruses are smallpox, measles, rabies, influenza, common cold, and poliomyelitis. Chickenpox and shingles are a linked pair of diseases now recognized to be caused by the same virus. As well as diseases in man many virus diseases are known in other animals. Myxomatosis of rabbits has been widely discussed since the post-war epidemics. Foot and mouth disease of domestic cattle, swine fever, and fowl pest are other virus diseases of great importance in agriculture. Viruses which attack insect larvae produce characteristic bundles of virus particles in polyhedral structures or in minute capsules. These polyhedral or capsular viruses usually cause death and may be used to control insect pests. The viruses which attack bacteria, the phages, usually cause the cells to break down completely into a liquid containing many new phage particles, a process termed lysis.

Viruses attacking animals are classified into groups which show similar features both in structure and in the disease which they cause, e.g. Influenza group, Pox group, Herpes group.

Transmission and reproduction

Minute doses of virus are capable of spreading infection and once an epidemic has built up, e.g. of foot and mouth disease, the virus concerned has amazing ability to spread from one place to another. Some animal viruses, such as those of influenza and measles, are normally very labile and survive outside their hosts for only a few hours, but others are extremely stable and withstand heat, cold, or drought which would destroy many proteins and bacteria. Antibiotics and many chemotherapeutic substances have no effect on viruses which are also resistant to many disinfectants. Oxidizing agents such as hydrogen peroxide and hypochlorites can be used to destroy them.

Some plant and animal viruses are transmitted and complete particles introduced into host cells by insect and other arthropod vectors, and even by dog-bite in the case of rabies. Other viruses may gain access to higher animals through the mouth and nose from dust, droplet infection, or contaminated food. In some diseases the particles appear to be carried into the body of the cell by pinocytosis but in other cases it is not clear how the infecting viruses pass through cell membranes, and whether only the nucleic acid fragment or this, together with part of its protein, may enter the host cytoplasm. Viral protein, if it enters the body of the cell, remains in the host cytoplasm, where, after a short period, called the *eclipse phase*, much new virus protein is formed and collects. The nucleic acid fragment enters the nucleus or nuclear body where it is replicated, and when the new viral nucleic acid particles leave the nucleus, virus protein quickly aggregates round them to make new, stable virions. During the eclipse phase, which is usually short, no virus particles can be seen in the cells, and they show no infectivity. Very soon afterwards the reproductive phase is evident and new virus particles are rapidly produced. Although only the core of the head of a phage virion enters the infected bacterium, both parts of the virus are synthesized and form into new, complete particles. Within 20 to 60 minutes one phage particle inside a bacterium may increase to 200 or more, when the bacterium, or what is left of it, bursts, liberating more phages which attack more bacteria, till a whole colony may be lysed, being reduced to a watery droplet full of bacteriophage.

Occasionally some phages have an extended eclipse phase, when the bacterial cells carry latent infection, which is called *temperate phage*, for many generations without sign or effect. Then spontaneously the temperate phage reverts to the vegetative phase and the bacterial colonies are lysed. *Latent viruses* occur commonly in both animals and plants which then carry an infection without showing any symptoms and so remain as a reservoir of the disease.

Inclusion bodies

As viruses multiply within the host's cells, large distinctive structures called *inclusion bodies* may appear in the cytoplasm or in the nucleus. These bodies may be from 1–30 μ diameter, and as they stain characteristically they are often of diagnostic importance, e.g. in rabies of the dog the presence of such structures in brain cells justifies presumptive diagnosis. The inclusion bodies appear to be intimately concerned with virus replication for some electron micrographs have shown them to contain numbers of virus particles. Small, multiple inclusions have been found in cells of hosts infected with smallpox and large inclusion bodies are characteristic of fowl-pox.

Interference

When organisms are inoculated with certain viruses they may become resistant to a second more virulent virus. The infections may be quite unrelated but the phenomenon usually is evident between similar viruses, e.g. between two strains of influenza or of the common cold. Occasionally two viruses may cause simultaneous but reduced infection, both multiplying at the same time in the same host, e.g. measles and poliomyelitis, or two potato viruses. It has, however, been shown that a soluble substance from some infected cells could cause the same interference with a second virus as the virus from which it was obtained. This product has been found to be a protein to which the name interferon was given. It is not antigenic. When a virus-infected cell produces interferon some of this diffuses to neighbouring cells to which it gives a measure of resistance against the disease, thus assisting the organism to recover. Interferon acts on or in the host cells preventing the synthesis of more virus particles. Weak viruses cause considerable interferon production while virulent strains result in very little interferon being formed.

Virus haemagglutination

Virus particles of the influenza group may attach themselves to the surface of some of the host's red blood cells often forming bridges between two cells and causing many to clump together. These erythrocytes are permanently damaged and no longer function but when they collapse they release the virus which can attack more cells. The haemagglutination reaction can be used to test the effectiveness of antibodies in prepared sera. If the antibody is mixed with the virus it normally combines with it and prevents any further virus reaction. The mixture when added to blood will cause agglutination only if effective virions remain.

Phage specificity and phage typing

Phages show close specificity for different strains of bacteria, often to a finer degree than is known for any other treatment of the bacterial cultures. The mechanism of specificity in most instances has been shown to lie in the attachment of the phage tail to the bacterial wall which is assumed to be due to the presence of complementary compounds which result in adsorption of the particle to the surface. The specificity of phages can be used to identify strains of bacteria which are not readily recognized by other means and for this purpose reference cultures of strains of bacteriophages are maintained in national collections and find important application in epidemiology.

Antiviral immunity in animals

In higher animals the same defence measures operate against infections with either viruses or bacteria. Both kinds of pathogen carry individual specific compounds called antigens on their surface which cause the host tissues, usually the lymphocytes of the blood, to synthesize and release into the blood serum antibodies which react with the antigen of the invading disease agent, preventing it from multiplying and allowing phago-cytes to remove it from the system. As virus particles inside a host cell cannot react with antibodies in the blood serum the latter must combine with virus particles before they enter susceptible cells. If a virus disease is already established antibodies will have little effect on its progress but as they usually remain in the blood for a long time they are very important in preventing a second attack. Thus it is possible to inoculate animals with a weak strain of a pathogenic virus which causes production of antibodies which will protect the organism from a further attack by a virulent strain. Such serious virus diseases as smallpox and poliomyelitis are now con-trolled in this way by vaccination.

Serology

This study concerns reactions between antigens and antibodies which result in a visible change such as a precipitation or an agglutination of cells. An antigen is any substance, usually a protein but occasionally a poly-saccharide, which, when injected into a suitable animal's body, stimulates the production in the blood serum of a specific protein antibody, usually a gamma-globulin, which combines with the antigen. The antigen may be part of the surface structure of a pathogen or it may be part of an organism completely foreign to the animal used. The serological reaction can be demonstrated if a small amount of prepared serum is added to the corre-sponding antigen. A line of white precipitate appears where antigen and antibody meet. The test is often carried out in petri dishes with a shallow layer of agar from which discs are cut to make a number of small wells. An extract of unknown cells or virus may be placed in a central well and a range of sera containing known antibodies placed in the surrounding wells. The colloidal solutions diffuse through the agar till they meet when specific substances react to give a line of precipitation. The method can be used for rapid identification of an unknown micro-organism or virus.

A refinement of the method has been developed by incubating the antibody gamma-globulin with a fluorescent dye with which it forms a stable compound without losing any of its serological properties. When it reacts with a specific organism or cell compound a line of strong fluorescence shows immediately where the two specific compounds meet. The method can be applied to the identification of strains of fungi using sera prepared from the blood of rabbits which have been injected with preparations of different strains or species. Young hyphal growths of an unknown fungus which cannot be recognized by any other method develop peripheral fluorescence when they meet a matching antibody which has been dyed (Plate 6E and F).

2

General Metabolic Processes

METABOLISM

All the complex activity which goes on inside the protoplasm of a living
cell while it carries out the functions of a living organism is covered by the
one word metabolism. The intricate systems of chemical reactions involved
are all controlled by enzymes, and include *catabolic* or breaking-down
reactions which release energy (i.e. are *exergonic*) and *anabolic* or
building-up reactions which require energy (i.e. are *endergonic*). Endergonic reactions cannot occur unless energy is supplied to them in a suitable
way. Photosynthetic organisms can use light energy for their primary
photosynthetic processes, but other endergonic reactions involve linkage
to some exergonic activity which supplies more energy than is actually
used. Such a system of coupled reactions will then function. Continued
research has unravelled some of the complex pathways of these linked
processes, many of which prove to be basic features of the metabolism of
all kinds of protoplasm. Probably the best known of these are the reactions
connected with respiration or the oxidation of glucose which is the main
exergonic process in living cells. Fungi and bacteria, however, carry out
some special changes peculiar to their own metabolism as well as the widely-
occurring general processes. Nearly all the reactions of metabolism are
coupled or linked in chains. Some examples are outlined below.

Synthesis of polysaccharides

Many organisms including fungi and bacteria build glycogen and other
polysaccharides from glucose, by an endergonic reaction. The commonly
occurring cytoplasmic compound adenosine triphosphate (ATP) is the

principal energy carrier in the cell because it readily forms adenosine di-phosphate (ADP) and free phosphate in an exergonic reaction, yet also it is readily regenerated in respiring cells. The breakdown of ATP is linked in living cells with many different endergonic reactions such as the formation of glycogen, the overall reaction for which is summarized as follows:

$$\text{glucose} + \text{ATP} \rightarrow \text{glycogen} + \text{ADP} + \text{free phosphate} + \text{energy}$$

In the presence of phosphorylase enzyme the ATP reacts with glucose to form glucose-1-phosphate (an ester of phosphoric acid with the glycosidic hydroxyl group). This transfer of phosphate also requires the presence of a magnesium or other divalent metal ion. Then the glucose-1-phosphate molecules react under enzymic action to form the polymer glycogen and free phosphate with liberation of a small surplus of energy. Some pre-formed glycogen is apparently also necessary in the system before more can be built up. Some polysaccharide synthesis may also involve the compounds uridine di- and triphosphate which are similar to ADP and ATP.

Most metabolic reactions are reversible and the synthesis of glycogen or starch as stored food in organisms is followed by the subsequent use of the substance which is broken down again to glucose. This breakdown is a hydrolysis reaction which is exergonic but which gives only a small energy yield per mole compared with the reaction:

$$\text{ATP} \rightarrow \text{ADP} + \text{phosphate} + \text{energy}$$

The terminal phosphate bond of the triphosphate is also broken down in a hydrolysis, but it is a high-energy bond which yields two to five times as much energy per mole as the hydrolysis of a glycoside, peptide or ordinary phosphate link, which are all low-energy bonds. Most organisms store large amounts of energy in substantial quantities of material such as glycogen, but the use of this in metabolic processes usually requires transforming it into high-energy bonds.

RESPIRATION

The key compound ATP is present in only very small amounts in living cells which are, however, able to re-form it quickly from ADP and free phosphate. This combination is linked to the exergonic process of oxidation of glucose which is the principal reaction of respiration. Oxidation of foodstuff is the essential protoplasmic method of liberating energy to drive all the endergonic processes of living cells. Oxidations characteristically liberate energy. When glucose is burnt it combines vigorously with oxygen of the air to form carbon dioxide and water and to give out heat. Such an exergonic reaction is often likened to a falling stone, which releases energy in its fall, and which can only be restored to activity if some force pulls it back again. Under the controlled conditions of a living cell, however, the falling stone reaction is tied to a number of smaller stones which are raised in succession, or perhaps rotated, as the first one falls with just enough weight to move the whole system gently.

The overall equation for aerobic respiration of glucose in living cells is the same as for burning:

$$C_6H_{12}O_6 + 6O_2 \rightarrow 6CO_2 + 6H_2O + \text{free energy}$$

In cytoplasm this process is carried out in a series of linked reactions which absorb some of the energy released at each step.

Oxidation and reduction are equal and opposite reactions. When compound A is oxidized the oxygen may come from another compound B which is then reduced. An equivalent change is brought about if hydrogen is removed from compound A and added to compound B, for in this way also compound A is oxidized and B is reduced. The controlled oxidation reactions of the cell proceed, in fact, by the step-wise removal of hydrogen from glucose, and the reduction of some other compound to which the hydrogen is added, and which is said to act as a hydrogen acceptor. As long as more energy is released in the removal of hydrogen from glucose (or its derivatives) than is taken up in reducing the hydrogen acceptor the oxidation reaction can proceed.

The cytoplasmic hydrogen acceptors are important because they can be oxidized in other linked reactions to which they give some of the energy they received from the oxidation of glucose, so that chains of oxidation-reduction reactions take place in living cells. The end of the chain in aerobic respiration is the reduction of the oxygen of the air to form water by the hydrogen carried down the various energy-releasing steps on its path from glucose.

Two of the most important hydrogen carriers are nicotinamide adenine dinucleotide (NAD) and nicotinamide adenine dinucleotide phosphate (NADP) which act similarly in becoming readily reduced when they absorb energy, and then readily re-oxidized when they give out this energy. Each compound contains in its molecule one molecule of nicotinamide (a vitamin of the B group), a compound which many organisms cannot synthesize for themselves and which therefore must be supplied to them. The very small amounts of it which are needed are nevertheless essential for normal metabolism. Reduced NAD or NADP may react with flavo-proteins which form oxidation-reduction systems, such as flavin adenine dinucleotide (FAD). Riboflavin, vitamin B_2, forms part of this molecule. In turn reduced FAD reacts with one of the cytochromes. These are iron-porphyrin compounds present in aerobically respiring cells, which in the reduced state through the activity of an oxidase enzyme are capable of reducing oxygen of the air to form water, becoming at the same time re-oxidized (Fig. 2.1).

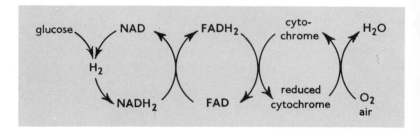

Fig. 2.1   Linked oxidation-reduction reactions of aerobic respiration.

The actual pattern of linked reactions is not universally identical, but one pathway for the oxidation of glucose, which has been traced in many plants and animals, and in various bacteria and fungi, goes in two separate series of reactions. Firstly, glucose is split in step-wise reactions which result in production of 2 molecules of pyruvic acid from each glucose molecule. This process which is anaerobic, requiring no oxygen, is called *glycolysis*. Secondly, the pyruvic acid is oxidized in a cycle of reactions, usually referred to as the *citric acid* or *tricarboxylic acid cycle* which is an aerobic process that can occur only in the presence of oxygen.

Glycolysis

The usual reaction steps for glycolysis are known as the **Embden-Meyerhof pathway** after the scientists who first traced the different stages. Glucose, an ordinarily stable compound, is converted first to fructosediphosphate, which is readily reactive, and which splits into 2 molecules each with a chain of 3 carbon atoms. These smaller molecules are converted to pyruvic acid. During these reactions energy is released. The process is illustrated in Fig. 2.2 and the complete series of reactions is given below, each being mediated by its own special enzyme.

1. glucose activated by reaction with ATP → glucopyranose-6-phosphate + ADP.
2. glucopyranose-6-phosphate $\rightarrow$ fructofuranose-6-phosphate.
3. fructofuranose-6-phosphate + ATP → fructofuranose-1-6-diphosphate + ADP.
4. fructofuranose-1-6-diphosphate → 1-phosphodihydroxyacetone + 3-phosphoglyceraldehyde (these are tautomeric, i.e. readily interchanging).

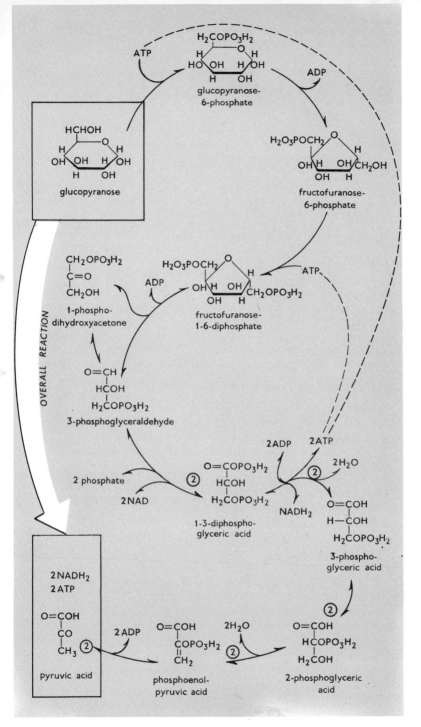

Fig. 2.2 Embden-Meyerhof pathway for glycolysis.

5. 2,3-phosphoglyceraldehyde + 2phosphate + 2NAD → 2,1-3-diphosphoglyceric acid + 2NADH$_2$.
6. 2,1-3-diphosphoglyceric acid + 2ADP → 2,3-phosphoglyceric acid + 2ATP + 2H$_2$O.
7. 2,3-phosphoglyceric acid → 2,2-phosphoglyceric acid.
8. 2,2-phosphoglyceric acid → 2phosphoenolpyruvic acid + 2H$_2$O.
9. 2phosphoenolpyruvic acid + 2ADP → 2pyruvic acid + 2ATP.

The total reaction then is:

$$\text{glucose} + 2\text{NAD} + 2\text{ADP} + 2\text{phosphate} \rightarrow$$
$$2\text{pyruvic acid} + 2\text{NADH}_2 + 2\text{ATP}$$

Citric acid or tricarboxylic acid cycle

Pyruvic acid formed by glycolysis is broken down by enzyme action to carbon dioxide and an acetyl group which is carried on co-enzyme A. The acetyl group combines with the 4-carbon compound oxaloacetic acid, which is normally present during aerobic respiration, and citric acid, with a chain of 6 carbon atoms, results. This undergoes a series of oxidation or hydrolysis changes during which energy is released. Hydrogen passes to the hydrogen acceptors in the cell, and carbon dioxide is given off, till oxaloacetic acid is reformed, so that the reactions continue in a cycle. The process is illustrated in Fig. 2.3 and the main series of reactions involved are listed below, each depending on its own specific enzyme.

1. pyruvic acid is decarboxylated to carbon dioxide and acetaldehyde which forms acetyl co-enzyme A.
2. acetyl co-enzyme A + oxaloacetic acid → citric acid + co-enzyme A (which reacts again with pyruvic acid).
3. citric acid → cis-aconitic acid + H$_2$O.
4. cis-aconitic acid + H$_2$O → isocitric acid.
5. isocitric acid + NADP → oxalosuccinic acid + NADPH$_2$.
6. oxalosuccinic acid → α-ketoglutaric acid + CO$_2$.
7. α-ketoglutaric acid + ADP + phosphate + NAD + H$_2$O → succinic acid + ATP + NADH$_2$ + CO$_2$.
8. succinic acid + FAD → fumaric acid + FADH$_2$.
9. fumaric acid + H$_2$O → malic acid.
10. malic acid + NAD → oxaloacetic acid + NADH$_2$.

The cycle is back to (2) and continues in the presence of oxygen which is used for re-oxidation of cytochrome which reacts with NADH$_2$ and FADH$_2$.

The overall result equals:

$$CH_3COCOOH + 5O \rightarrow 3CO_2 + 2H_2O + \text{energy sufficient}$$

pyruvic acid

to build up about 15ATP from ADP and phosphate.

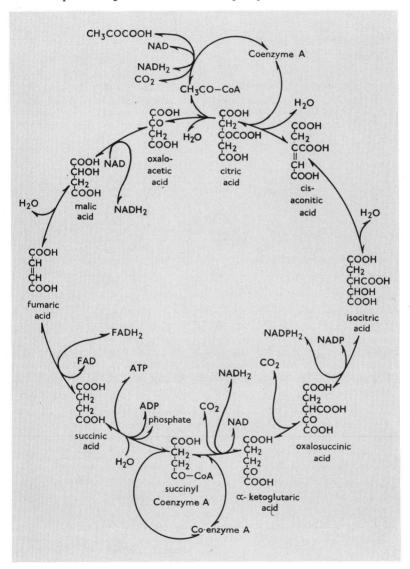

Fig. 2.3 Citric acid cycle showing reactions followed in oxidative degradation of pyruvic acid.

It is clear that the yield of energy from glycolysis, the anaerobic process, is small compared with the yield from the aerobic conversion of pyruvic acid. At any one time only part of the glucose broken down may become completely oxidized because pyruvic acid and many of the compounds of the citric acid cycle are important intermediates used in other metabolic reactions.

Pentose phosphate pathway

Although the Embden-Meyerhof pathway of glycolysis is commonly followed another route for the breakdown of glucose, known as the pentose phosphate pathway, occurs in many organisms and is of considerable importance in fungi and bacteria. It is illustrated in outline in Fig. 2.4 and suggested reactions are given below.

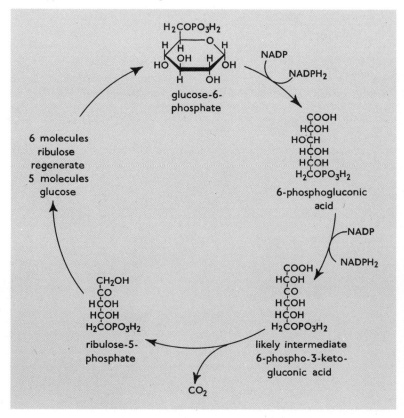

Fig. 2.4 Outline diagram of pentose phosphate pathway of carbohydrate metabolism.

1. glucose + ATP → glucose-6-phosphate + ADP.
2. glucose-6-phosphate + NADP → 6-phosphogluconolactone + $NADPH_2$.
3. 6-phosphogluconolactone + H_2O → 6-phosphogluconic acid.
4. 6-phosphogluconic acid + NADP → ribulose-5-phosphate + $NADPH_2$ + CO_2.
5. ribulose-5-phosphate → C_3 fragment + C_2 fragment (e.g. glyceraldehyde-3-phosphate + glycolaldehyde).
   The C_3 and C_2 fragments may be recombined to regenerate glucose.
   6 molecules ribulose-5-phosphate → 5 molecules glucose phosphate

The overall result is then:

$$\text{glucose-6-phosphate} + 12NADP + 6H_2O \rightarrow$$
$$6CO_2 + 12NADPH_2 + 1\text{phosphate}$$

The complete reaction can in some circumstances proceed aerobically with the H_2 of $NADPH_2$ being passed through a complex series of steps, reacting eventually through cytochrome with oxygen of the air, but commonly $NADPH_2$ is reoxidized during synthetic events. The energy released by the oxidation of one molecule of glucose is sufficient to form approximately 35ATP from ADP and phosphate.

In the absence of oxygen however, the C_3 and C_2 fragments may react as follows:

$$\text{glyceraldehyde-3-phosphate} \rightarrow \text{pyruvic acid}$$
$$\text{glycolaldehyde} \rightarrow \text{ethanol}$$

Entner-Doudoroff pathway

A third system for the breakdown of glucose is named after these two scientists. It is followed in the respiration of a number of bacteria. Suggested stages are as follows:

1. glucose-6-phosphate + NADP → 6-phosphogluconolactone + $NADPH_2$.
2. 6-phosphogluconolactone → 2-keto-3-deoxyphosphogluconic acid.
3. 2-keto-3-deoxyphosphogluconic acid → pyruvic acid + glyceraldehyde-3-phosphate.
4. glyceraldehyde-3-phosphate (by Embden-Meyerhof pathway) → pyruvic acid.

A diagram outlining these changes is given in Fig. 2.5.

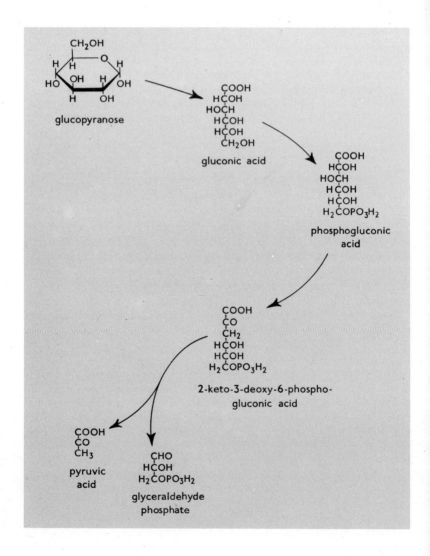

Fig. 2.5 Entner-Doudoroff pathway of glycolysis.

The three systems described for splitting glucose may be summarized:

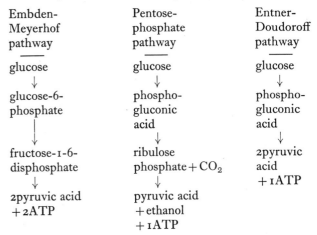

Embden-Meyerhof pathway	Pentose-phosphate pathway	Entner-Doudoroff pathway
glucose	glucose	glucose
↓	↓	↓
glucose-6-phosphate	phospho-gluconic acid	phospho-gluconic acid
↓	↓	↓
fructose-1-6-disphosphate	ribulose phosphate + CO_2	2pyruvic acid + 1ATP
↓	↓	
2pyruvic acid + 2ATP	pyruvic acid + ethanol + 1ATP	

In each case the pyruvic acid formed may undergo further changes as it fills many roles in metabolism.

AEROBIC AND ANAEROBIC ORGANISMS

The citric acid cycle definitely requires oxygen to function, but glycolysis can proceed as long as there is a supply of a suitable hydrogen acceptor. Organisms which carry out the complete breakdown of glucose must have a supply of oxygen and are either strict *aerobes* using oxygen gas, or organisms taking oxygen from either sulphate or nitrate ions. Without oxygen their metabolism comes to a halt. Some organisms, however, are able to dispose of the hydrogen produced in glycolysis in other ways and thus can live in the absence of oxygen. *Facultative anaerobes* are organisms which can respire either using oxygen or without it, but when supplied with oxygen they grow better because the complete oxidation of glucose yields much more energy per mole than glycolysis. Yeast is a good example and many other fungi are also facultative anaerobic organisms. *Indifferent* organisms are those which do not use atmospheric oxygen but which grow quite well in its presence without using it, e.g. the denitrifying bacteria and the lactic acid organisms. The *strict anaerobes* are poisoned by air or oxygen and are unable to grow in its presence. They are able to use only materials other than oxygen as hydrogen acceptors.

FERMENTATION OR ANAEROBIC REACTIONS

In the absence of air, facultative anaerobes, indifferent organisms or strict anaerobes may use a variety of compounds as hydrogen acceptors and so accumulate a variety of end products. A substance frequently formed by fermentation (anaerobic respiration) of glucose is ethanol which is produced by the facultative organism, yeast, as well as by many other fungi and bacteria which may use acetaldehyde formed from pyruvic acid as a hydrogen acceptor.

$$CH_3COCOOH \rightarrow CH_3CHO + CO_2$$
pyruvic acid   acetaldehyde

$$CH_3CHO + NADH_2 \rightarrow CH_3CH_2OH + NAD$$
ethanol

Alternatively through the splitting of ribulose-phosphate ethanol is produced from glycolaldehyde. In either of these cases carbon dioxide is formed as well as ethanol.

The indifferent lactic organisms use pyruvic acid as a hydrogen acceptor and form lactic acid, as do the muscles of animals when they work very rapidly and temporarily exhaust the supply of oxygen.

$$CH_3COCOOH + NADH_2 \rightarrow CH_3CHOHCOOH + NAD$$
lactic acid

Organisms which produce only lactic acid from fermentation of glucose do not produce any carbon dioxide. In fermentation where carbon dioxide is formed as well as ethanol, glycolysis usually proceeds by the pentose phosphate pathway. Some bacteria, however, are able to use carbon dioxide as a hydrogen acceptor and produce formic acid or methane.

$$CO_2 + NADH_2 \rightarrow HCOOH + NAD$$
formic acid

$$CO_2 + 4NADH_2 \rightarrow CH_4 + 2H_2O + 4NAD$$
methane

The denitrifying bacteria use nitrate as a hydrogen acceptor and produce nitrogen gas.

$$2NO_3 + 6NADH_2 \rightarrow N_2 + 6H_2O + 6NAD$$

Some of the strict anaerobes use amino acids as hydrogen acceptors and also decarboxylate them, producing highly toxic amines. A few anaerobic bacteria actually produce hydrogen gas. External conditions, particularly oxygen pressure, temperature and pH, influence the course of fermentation. In the identification of bacteria it is important to examine how they ferment different sugars and what compounds they produce under defined conditions. Some of the possibilities from fermentation of glucose are indicated in Table 2.1.

Table 2.1 Examples of Fermentations

	carbon dioxide	hydrogen	formic acid	acetic acid	propionic acid	butyric acid	lactic acid	succinic acid	ethanol	isopropanol	butanol	glycerol	butylene glycol	acetone	Type of fermentation
Saccharomyces cerevisiae	+								+						alcoholic
Streptococcus lactis							+								simple lactic
Lactobacillus brevis	+			+			+		+			+			mixed lactic
Propionibacterium sp.	+			+	+			+							propionic
Escherichia coli	+	+	+	+			+	+	+	+					CDT or colon-dysentery-typhoid
Aerobacter aerogenes	+	+	+						+				+		CDT or colon-dysentery-typhoid
Salmonella typhi			+	+			+	+	+						CDT or colon-dysentery-typhoid
Clostridium butyricum	+	+		+		+									butyric
Clostridium acetobutylicum	+	+		+		+			+		+			+	butyl
Clostridium butylicum	+	+		+		+				+	+				isopropyl

CARBON DIOXIDE FIXATION

In many heterotrophic organisms some carbon dioxide, though often only a small amount, is necessary for growth and is usually fixed by either of the two following reactions:

I. $$CH_3COCOOH + CO_2 \rightarrow COOHCH_2COCOOH$$
pyruvic acid — oxaloacetic acid

Carbon dioxide is combined directly with pyruvic acid to form oxalo-acetic acid.

2. $CH_3COCOOH + CO_2 + NADPH_2 \rightarrow$

$$COOHCHOHCH_2COOH + NADP$$
malic acid

Pyruvic acid reacts with carbon dioxide and reduced NADP to form malic acid.

Either reaction provides a supply of organic acid which may be needed for amino-acid synthesis when the supply from the respiratory cycle is insufficient. This fixation of carbon dioxide is quite distinct from that which takes place in photosynthesis (p. 56).

FAT SYNTHESIS

Fats are compounds of fatty acids and glycerol. The glycerol may be produced from dihydroxyacetone phosphate which is formed in glycolysis.

$$
\begin{array}{ccc}
CH_2OPO_3H_2 & CH_2OPO_3H_2 & CH_2OH \\
| & | & | \\
C=O & CHOH & CHOH \\
| & | & | \\
CH_2OH \longrightarrow & CH_2OH \longrightarrow & CH_2OH + phosphate
\end{array}
$$

dihydroxy   glycerol-1-   glycerol
acetone phosphate phosphate

The fatty-acid units are produced by condensation of acetyl units on acetyl co-enzyme A, and their progressive hydrogenation. Acetyl coenzyme A which is a starting point for fatty-acid synthesis may equally be an end point in fatty-acid degradation. It may also be the last compound of glycolysis or the beginning of glucose synthesis. This connecting link allows living cells readily to interconvert fats and carbohydrates.

SYNTHESIS OF AMINO ACIDS

The fungi and bacteria which are able to live on a medium of mineral salts, if given a supply of carbohydrate, synthesize amino acids using inorganic nitrogen compounds. Either they absorb ammonium ions directly from the medium or they absorb nitrate, or possibly nitrite, which they then reduce in the cell to ammonium. There are probably two ways in which the ammonium is incorporated into organic compounds. *Firstly*, and of most importance, is the well-established reaction with α-ketoglutaric acid to form glutamic acid and then glutamine:

1.

$$
\begin{array}{lcccl}
\underset{\text{α-ketoglutaric acid}}{\begin{array}{l}COOH \\ | \\ C\!=\!O \\ | \\ CH_2 \\ | \\ CH_2 \\ | \\ COOH \end{array}}
& \begin{array}{c} NH_3 \\ \searrow \\ \rightarrow \\ \nearrow \\ H_2 \\ \text{from reduced co-enzyme} \end{array}
& \underset{\text{glutamic acid}}{\begin{array}{l} COOH \\ | \\ CHNH_2 \!\rightarrow \\ | \\ CH_2 \\ | \\ CH_2 \\ | \\ COOH \end{array}}
& \begin{array}{c} H_2O \\ \nearrow \\ \rightarrow \\ NH_3 \\ \searrow \end{array}
& \underset{\text{glutamine}}{\begin{array}{l} COOH \\ | \\ CHNH_2 \\ | \\ CH_2 \\ | \\ CH_2 \\ | \\ C\!=\!O \\ | \\ NH_2 \end{array}}
\end{array}
$$

Secondly, of less importance and less well-established, is the direct reaction with fumaric acid to form aspartic acid and then asparagine:

2.

$$
\begin{array}{lcccl}
\underset{\text{fumaric acid}}{\begin{array}{l} COOH \\ | \\ CH \\ \| \\ CH \\ | \\ COOH \end{array}}
& \begin{array}{c} NH_3 \\ \searrow \\ \rightarrow \end{array}
& \underset{\text{aspartic acid}}{\begin{array}{l} COOH \\ | \\ CHNH_2 \\ | \\ CH_2 \\ | \\ COOH \end{array}}
& \begin{array}{c} NH_3 \\ \searrow \\ \rightarrow \end{array}
& \underset{\text{asparagine}}{\begin{array}{l} COOH \\ | \\ CHNH_2 \!\rightarrow H_2O \\ | \\ CH_2 \\ | \\ C\!=\!O \\ | \\ NH_2 \end{array}}
\end{array}
$$

Glutamic acid and aspartic acid are the two primary amino acids formed by fungi and bacteria. The corresponding amides, glutamine and asparagine, are known to move through cell membranes more readily than the amino acids, and also they serve to store extra ammonia. Once the ammonia has been converted to an amino group of either of these acids it is readily transferred by a transaminase enzyme to the keto analogue of any other amino acid, and any of the 20 different amino acids commonly found may be formed in this way.

$$
\underset{\text{glutamic acid}}{\begin{array}{l} COOH \\ | \\ CHNH_2 \\ | \\ CH_2 \\ | \\ CH_2 \\ | \\ COOH \end{array}}
+ \underset{\substack{\text{pyruvic} \\ \text{acid}}}{\begin{array}{l} COOH \\ | \\ CO \\ | \\ CH_3 \end{array}}
\rightarrow \underset{\text{alanine}}{\begin{array}{l} COOH \\ | \\ CHNH_2 \\ | \\ CH_3 \end{array}}
+ \underset{\text{α-ketoglutaric acid}}{\begin{array}{l} COOH \\ | \\ C\!=\!O \\ | \\ CH_2 \\ | \\ CH_2 \\ | \\ COOH \end{array}}
$$

The nitrogen-fixing organisms which are described in the section on soil (p. 70) incorporate nitrogen by the same pathway. First molecular nitrogen is reduced to ammonia which is then combined with either α-ketoglutaric acid or fumaric acid.

PROTEIN SYNTHESIS

Each protein molecule consists of a unique linear sequence of different amino acids linked together by combination of the amino group of one and the carboxyl group of the next to give a peptide linkage. The amino acids are joined by the adjacent functional groups with the remainder of the molecule lying approximately at right angles to the peptide chain. One particular protein may have a molecule built from fifty to several thousand amino acids, forming a long and complex chain which becomes bent, spiralled or rolled into its own characteristic shape. The essential properties of each protein depend on the order in which the individual amino acids are arranged. If we consider twenty different amino acids combined in strings of just one hundred, the possible number of different combinations is exceedingly large, quite sufficient to allow each species of organism to have many characteristic kinds of protein molecules. How this intricate complexity may be controlled has been indicated by recent research on nucleic acids.

Nucleic acids

The deoxyribonucleic acids (DNA) are the vital chemical compounds in the chromosomes which carry the hereditary instructions of each organism. One single gene is believed to consist of a single segment of a DNA macromolecule. The ribonucleic acids (RNA) which are found both in the nucleus and in the cytoplasm show some similarities in structure to DNA. The nucleic acids control the synthesis of each different kind of protein in a way which is outlined below.

Both DNA and RNA consist of long slender macromolecules built of small repeating units called *nucleotides*, each of which is a combination of a pentose phosphate and an organic heterocyclic base. In DNA the pentose is always deoxyribose (2-deoxy-D-erythro-pentose) only, and in RNA it is D-ribose. The organic bases in nucleic acids are of two types and predominantly of six kinds as follows:

Purines	*Pyrimidines*	
adenine	cytosine	methylcytosine
guanine	uracil	thymine
		(methyluracil)

Fig. 2.6   (a) Diagram of structure of DNA molecule. (b) Matching of corresponding bases thymine and adenine. (c) Linkage of cytosine and guanine.

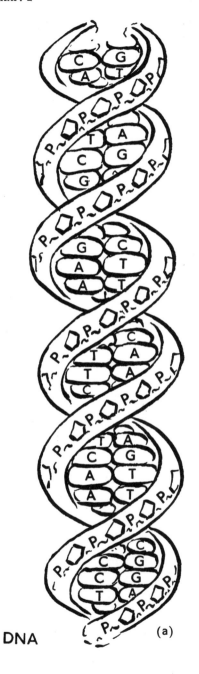

DNA   (a)

nucleotide chain

thymine

adenine

nucleotide chain

(b)

nucleotide chain

cytosine

guanine

nucleotide chain

(c)

RNA normally consists of nucleotides containing the four bases, adenine, guanine, cytosine and uracil, while DNA usually contains nucleotides of adenine, guanine, cytosine and thymine, although cytosine may be replaced by methylcytosine or, in some bacteriophages, by hydroxymethylcytosine.

The DNA macromolecule consists of a double strand of two parallel pentose-phosphate chains wound in the form of a regular helix or spiral (Fig. 2.6a). The organic bases attached to each pentose-phosphate unit are orientated within the helix and approach one another in the centre where there are hydrogen bonds between them (Fig. 2.6). Each base requires a definite opposite partner, so that the composition of the first strand determines the composition of the twin strand. Thus one can understand how the double coil could, conceivably, replicate itself. If the two strands uncoil in the presence of a supply of more nucleotides, each base on each separate coil would attract its opposite number, enabling the synthesis of two new double coils from the original one, the new pair of double coils exactly replicating the original double coil. A single DNA macromolecule may be 10,000 nucleotide units long, so the chemical problem of working out the sequence of the base pairs along such a chain is obviously difficult, but this sequence is of very great importance since it is the basis of the genetic code. The possible number of proteins is almost unimaginably large but the possible total of different DNA macromolecules is very much larger still.

RNA chains are shorter, the macromolecules being smaller, of comparable size to protein molecules. Several types are known. Messenger RNA, believed to be in single coils, is synthesized on the chromosomal DNA from which it carries a gene message to a ribosome. Transfer RNA is the smallest type of this macromolecule with 80–100 nucleotides; it is coiled on itself in three places with single loops between so that it takes up a 'clover-leaf' form. Each kind of transfer RNA bears a code in an order of bases which binds one particular amino acid. Ribosomes, the cell organelles which are the site of protein synthesis, are formed from two separate unequal particles, each consisting of RNA and protein. These originate in the nucleolus from where they migrate to the cytoplasm. When the smaller ribosomal particle becomes associated with a formylmethionyl tRNA, in the presence of certain necessary factors such as the requisite enzymes and certain charged ions, it then can bind to the larger particle to form a functional ribosome. This then associates with a unit of messenger RNA and commences protein synthesis, building on to the formylmethionate by holding successive transfer RNAs with their amino acids according to the code of the bases on the messenger RNA. It has been suggested that the long messenger RNA molecule moves through a slot between the two parts of the ribosome as its message is transcribed and that the spent end of the messenger RNA is immediately broken down by ribonuclease. Enzyme action condenses the amino acids in order, so that they build up in a polypeptide chain attached to the ribosome. When the code for the end of the molecule is reached the protein is in some way shed from the ribosome-messenger RNA complex and moves to the site in the cell where it is required.

Nucleotides

Apart from their presence in nucleic acids, several nucleotides occur free in living cells where they play an essential role in metabolism. Important compounds include adenylic acid, from which both adenosine di- and triphosphate, ADP and ATP are derived; nicotinamide adenine dinucleotide, NAD, and its phosphate, NADP; riboflavin phosphate; co-enzyme A; and flavin adenine dinucleotide, FAD.

THE MECHANISM OF METABOLISM: ENZYMES

A few processes which occur generally in protoplasm have been outlined in the previous sections. The chemical reactions of metabolism, however, are multifarious, resulting in all the different compounds that make up the organism as well as in the continuation of the processes going on within it. Many changes may occur simultaneously either in continuing chains of reactions or in complex cycles, but each single step is under control and the orderly sequence is carried out smoothly in the living cell. These chemical processes are all brought about by the action or activity of *biological catalysts* or enzymes. These are protein compounds, some of which are highly specific and bring about only one reaction, while others are active on one class of compound bringing about a certain type of reaction. A single living cell may possibly contain 1,000 or more different enzymes.

Each enzyme molecule may be compared with a key of special pattern which fits the molecules of its own specific reaction. The reacting molecules become adsorbed temporarily on the surface of the enzyme, or even very briefly combined with it so that they are brought close together. This does not happen all over the enzyme molecule but only at active centres, or just at one active centre on the molecule. It is also necessary at least in some enzymic reactions for a large electric charge, such as that carried by a magnesium or phosphate ion, to be close enough to cause distortion of the structure of the reacting groups. As soon as these have formed a new compound or compounds they are immediately shed from the enzyme which then acts again in the same way. Thus a few enzyme molecules may act in a short space of time on a large amount of material, called the *substrate*, so that small amounts of enzyme may have a large and often rapid effect. Although enzymes are theoretically unchanged by the reactions which they promote, they nevertheless consist of proteins which are compounds readily susceptible to change. Some are more stable and have a longer period of activity than others. Characteristically they act reversibly and bring each reaction quickly to an equilibrium, but if one component is removed from a system the enzyme reaction will continue in one direction; and, as mentioned in the earlier paragraphs on metabolism, as long as a system of linked reactions is exergonic it will continue to operate.

Like all proteins, enzymes are sensitive to pH and heat. Many are not solely proteins but have comparatively small molecules, called **prosthetic groups**, associated with them. Such groups often contain a transition metal atom such as cobalt, copper, molybdenum, zinc, or the 'group' may consist only of the metal atom. These are some of the well-known trace elements of nutrition, required by organisms in exceedingly small amounts and yet without them the organisms cannot function at all because they cannot carry out some vital enzymic reaction. Neither the enzyme protein nor the special group has any activity by itself. Many of the vitamins can also function effectively as prosthetic groups, commonly called in this instance co-enzymes, because they serve as carriers during the enzymic reactions. Like the trace elements they are required in very small amounts for the normal functions of those organisms which are unable to synthesize what they need for themselves. Other vitamins, especially of the B group, may form part of the enzyme proper, or its prosthetic group.

Enzymes in general are named by adding **-ase** to the substance or groups on which they act, or to the class of reaction they catalyse. Examples of some main kinds of enzymes are:

1 **Hydrolases** which bring about breakdown by hydrolysis. As hydrolysis reactions are exergonic, these normally proceed to completion. Examples are the digestive enzymes: **cellulase** which hydrolyses cellulose; **amylase** which hydrolyses starch (amylum); **lipase** which hydrolyses lipids or fats; **peptidase** which hydrolyses the peptide bond of proteins.
2 **Phosphorylases** attack similar bonds to those broken by hydrolases, but act in the presence of phosphate which is added to one of the fractional molecules to form a phosphate ester. As little energy change is involved these reactions are freely reversible.
3 **Transferases** are enzymes which transfer some special group or radical from one molecule to another, such as the transfer of an amino group to form different amino acids, or of phosphate groups to form different phosphate esters.
4 **Decarboxylases** split off carbon dioxide from organic acids, especially from those with a RCOCOOH or RCHOHCOOH configuration.
5 **Oxidases** and **dehydrogenases** are the enzymes which bring about the important reactions of respiration. Most dehydrogenases require hydrogen carriers (p. 28) as co-enzymes. The enzymes which promote the final reaction with oxygen gas are oxidases.

6 *Lysozymes* are enzymes which catalyse the hydrolysis of cell substances and which may be present in most cells in minute vacuoles or in protected 'packets'. They may serve to remove metabolic compounds the function of which is finished. Some secretions of higher animals, especially man, contain lysozyme capable of digesting bacterial cell walls, and thus of halting bacterial infection in the same way as penicillin. The complete molecular structure of lysozyme from tears and nasal secretion has now been elucidated.

Besides these well-known kinds of enzymes, a further group may be recognized associated with the uptake of ions by the cell, a process which shows some characteristics of enzyme reactions. These *permeases* are active units resembling enzymes, present in the semi-permeable surface membranes across which they transfer nutrient substances which cannot otherwise penetrate the cell.

The enzyme *invertase* or *sucrase* which can be extracted from yeast cells is an example of a specific enzyme. It is adapted solely to the hydrolysis of a β-D-fructofuranoside link and so acts on sucrose to give fructose and glucose. It may hydrolyse other di- or trisaccharides containing β-fructofuranose. Some other fungi yield a different specific sucrase enzyme which acts solely on an α-glucoside link. This also hydrolyses sucrose to glucose and fructose but cannot act on other compounds unless they also have an exposed α-glucose unit.

Although enzymes can be prepared *in vitro* in colloidal solutions, and are secreted copiously by some fungi and bacteria as such, many appear to be localized within living cells where they are carried on different minute cell structures such as mitochondria, ribosomes and the cytoplasmic membranes. In this way they are separated in living cells where many enzyme reactions proceed harmoniously at the same time and where, in order to produce their complicated results, they must operate in a set sequence. The enzymes concerned in glycolysis seem to occur in solution in the cytoplasm where this process takes place. The reactions of aerobic respiration, on the other hand, are all located in the mitochondria.

3

Physiology of Growth and Development

GROWTH

This results primarily in an irreversible increase in size of a cell, an organism or a colony, and secondarily in an increase in numbers of cells or organisms, and also in an increase of fresh and dry weight. The increase depends on the supply of nutrients, physical conditions such as temperature, and on the organism's constitution and stage of development.

When unicellular organisms are cultured in liquid media under satisfactory conditions growth measured by cell numbers shows three phases (Fig. 3.1). When first inoculated into new media, cells take several hours to adapt themselves and during this time, called the **lag phase**, no growth occurs. Then rapid growth follows with regular division of all the cells present so that a graph of the logarithm of cell numbers against time is a straight line. This period is named the **log phase**. Fairly abruptly this free cell division ceases and the culture passes to a **stationary phase**. In a closed system this is brought about by changes in pH, exhaustion of some nutrient or accumulation of some retarding agent. If cells from a log phase of growth are used for an inoculum the log phase continues and there is no lag phase. By maintaining good conditions of growth by continuously adding fresh medium, the log phase may be maintained for long periods.

It is possible to determine from the slope of the growth curve the log phase **generation time**, i.e. how frequently the cells divide, which in any culture is determined mainly by the nutrients and the temperature (Table 3.1). It has been found for some organisms that a moderate reduction in temperature will prevent cell division while only reducing the rate

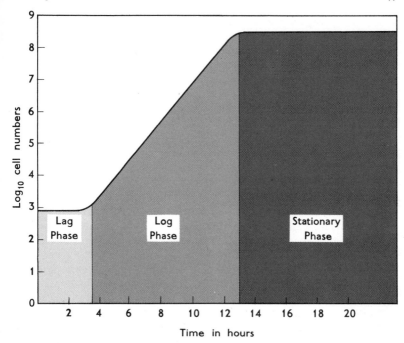

Fig. 3.1   Phases of growth as shown by increase in bacterial cell numbers in liquid culture.

of cell growth. Thus if a culture has been held for a period at a low temperature then, once a favourable temperature is restored, all cells divide synchronously and continue to divide together as long as log phase is maintained. With such *synchronized cultures* many special studies are possible. It has been found, for example, that the cell mass increases

Table 3.1   Generation Time of some Organisms under Optimum Conditions

Escherichia coli	20 minutes
Mycobacterium tuberculosis	18 hours
Saccharomyces cerevisiae	2 hours
Schizosaccharomyces pombe	4 hours

regularly, but that the synthesis of nuclear material (DNA) is cyclical, increasing rapidly just before or at cell division.

Fungal cultures on solid media show the same three stages of growth. The stationary phase in fungi is usually initiated by production of poisons or **staling compounds**. These latter may be some simple metabolic by-products which, however, inhibit further growth. Fungi vary greatly in their sensitivity to staling compounds, and in their ability to produce them, which is also affected by the nutrients available. Some fungi grow freely in cultures without showing symptoms of staling.

PHYSICAL FACTORS AFFECTING GROWTH

Temperature

This has a marked effect on fungi and bacteria though different organisms have different optimal temperatures. **Psychrophils** are organisms with optima lower than 20°C, some of which will continue to grow slowly at very low temperatures, e.g. many marine organisms and those which cause spoilage in cold stores. **Mesophils** (including most micro-organisms) have optima between 20 and 45°C. **Thermophils** have optima above 45°C and include fungi and bacteria of composts, fermenting haystacks and hot springs. Some of these exceptional organisms survive and even thrive at temperatures sufficiently high to kill most fungi and bacteria. Thermophilic micro-organisms examined from rotting maize which reached a temperature of 58°C included *Thermomyces lanuginosus*, *Mucor pusillus* and *Rhizomucor* sp. True thermophils are unable to grow at temperatures below 20°C. The temperature range for vegetative growth of some organisms is given in Table 3.2.

Table 3.2   Cardinal Temperatures (°C) for Vegetative Growth of some Organisms

Organism	Minimum	Optimum	Maximum
Clostridium thermocellum	50	60	68
Thermomyces lanuginosus	28–32	45–50	58–60
Rhizomucor sp.	25–30	45–50	60–61
Mucor pusillus	21–23	45–50	50–58
Chaetomium sp.	25	40–50	62
Escherichia coli	10	37	45
Mycobacterium tuberculosis	30	37	40
Saccharomyces cerevisiae	1–3	28	40
Fusarium caeruleum	5	20	30
Cladosporium herbarum	−6	unknown	20

Aeration

This is important in some liquid cultures, but on solid substrates in petri dishes the requirements of fungi and bacteria for oxygen do not exceed the supply. Some *carbon dioxide* is important, not only for the autotrophs which use it for synthesis of carbohydrates (p. 56), but also for many heterotrophs (p. 39).

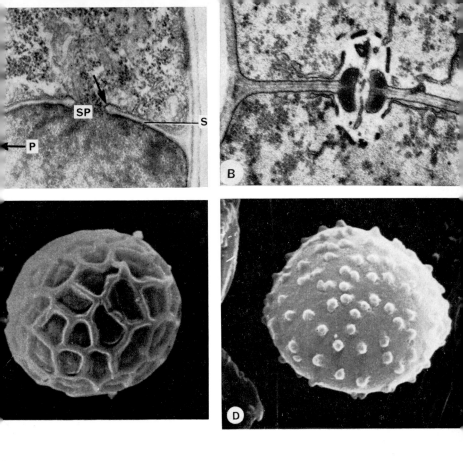

Plate 3 (**A**) Electron micrograph of a longitudinal section of a hypha of *Acremoniella velata* illustrating layered wall and septum (S) with one central septal pore (SP). Note (arrowed) swollen part of septum (double-layered structure of plasmalemma (P)) where the pore is formed. (From Jones, D., *Trans. Br. mycol. Soc.* **51**, 518, Pl. 37, Fig. 6) ×41,400. (**B**) Dolipore septum of *Coprinus lagopus*. ×20,000. (From Burnett, J. H. (1968) *Fundamentals of Mycology*, Pl. III, Fig. 1. Arnold, London.) (**C**) Scanning electron micrograph of brand spore (teliospore) of *Tilletia caries*. Note ridged hexagonal-pentagonal pattern of surface. ×3,150. (**D**) Scanning electron micrograph of brand spore of *Ustilago avenae*. Note wart-like protuberances on surface. ×8,850. (C and D from Jones, D., *Trans. Br. mycol. Soc.* **51**, 610, Pl. 45, Figs. 1 and 4.)

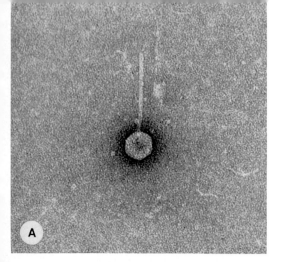

Plate 4 (**A**) (*left*) Original
micrograph of phage of *Bacillus*
terium. (By courtesy of Raynor
Bedford College.) ×120,000. (**B**) (
Cell from a carnation leaf showin
different viruses in one cell. Ca
mottle (28 nm diameter polyhedro
nation latent (650 nm filame
carnation etched ring virus complex
sphere component). ×130,000. (
graph M. Hollings by courtesy
Glasshouse Crops Research S
Rustington.)

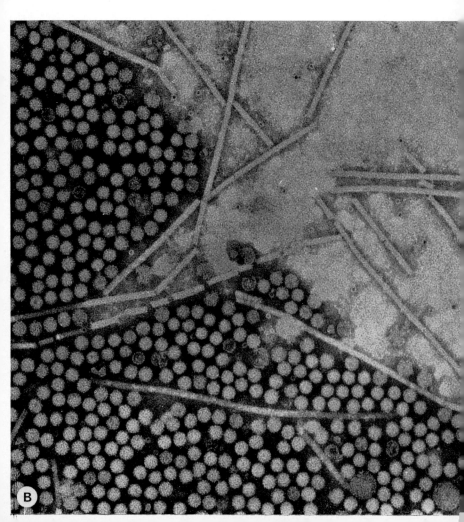

Light

For the photosynthetic autotrophs light is necessary, but otherwise has little obvious effect on the *growth* of the majority of bacteria and fungi though it may have a very important effect on the shedding of spores and on the maturation of fungi, which is discussed below. Bacteria and many other living cells are susceptible to ultra-violet light (also X-rays) which readily kills them. Exposure to sub-lethal doses may cause mutations. Ultra-violet light is often useful for sterilization.

Gravity

This provokes a sensitive response in many fungal structures carrying air-borne spores. The precision with which the fruiting bodies of many higher fungi are orientated is conspicuous and in many examples has been shown to be due to gravity. Some small toadstools, such as species of *Mycena*, if left lying in a covered dish, will turn their caps up within 1 or 2 hours so that the gills once more are exactly vertical (Fig. 3.2).

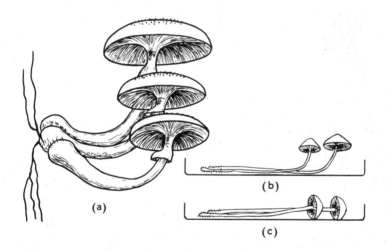

Fig. 3.2   Effect of gravity on fungi: (a) *Armillaria mellea* sporophores growing from a vertical tree trunk ($\times\frac{1}{2}$); (b and c) *Mycena rubromarginata* sporophores with caps turned up 4 hours after being placed flat in a dish ($\times\frac{1}{2}$).

DIFFERENTIATION, SPORE FORMATION AND GERMINATION

After unicellular organisms have grown to maximum size they divide and the two daughter cells repeat the same process, but for some species of bacteria a period under a particular set of conditions may induce changes in the type of growth. Some species develop L-forms (p. 8) in the presence of penicillin. In general unfavourable conditions for bacteria may induce pleomorphism (p. 8), and return to favourable conditions may allow a reversal to normal growth. However, little is yet known of what stimulates or controls the changes in form of bacteria.

Endospores, which are formed by species of the two genera *Clostridium* and *Bacillus*, are distinct in that one of their major constituents **dipicolinic acid** is not present in vegetative cells. They also have a higher calcium content than growing cells. Endospores are more resistant to heat, cold and disinfectants than almost any other kind of living cell. The species capable of forming endospores may produce them after a period of log phase growth, or when nutrients are exhausted, but starvation does not induce spore formation. Fatty acids have been shown to inhibit their development. Endospores contain fewer enzymes than vegetative cells and those present resemble the enzymes of the thermophilic organisms in being heat-stable. Once formed, bacterial endospores remain dormant for long periods and do not germinate until their dormancy is broken. Some require a short period of 'heat shock' or contact with some chemical substance, which stimulates uptake of water and causes bursting of the spore wall and activity of respiratory enzymes, before vegetative growth is resumed.

The vegetative growth of simple branching hyphae with which a typical fungal colony begins is usually followed by **differentiation**, which involves the development of cells or structures different from those formed earlier. The appearance of special reproductive organs and cells is the most conspicuous change in a growing fungus, and much experimental work has been done to determine conditions favouring asexual or sexual spore formation, or both, by various fungi in culture. Some, e.g. *Monilinia fructigena*, are strongly influenced by *light*, so that if grown in alternating light and dark they develop banded colonies showing sporulating rings which have received a light stimulus alternating with purely vegetative growth in the dark.

Under conditions favouring rapid growth many fungi continue to grow vegetatively, but a sudden change of a well-grown mycelium to less favourable conditions, particularly of food supply, will often induce production of spores. Some fungi have special nutritional requirements beyond those needed for vegetative growth before they can form spores. For some, addition of phosphate esters will stimulate immediate spore production; others require traces of certain metals which are normally present, but if they are withheld sporulation is prevented. *Aspergillus niger* can form conidia only in the presence of traces of molybdenum and other metals, and moreover the amount of typical black conidia formed is directly proportional to the amounts of metal present at trace levels (as low as hundredths of a part per million). Thus growth of the fungus can be used to assay traces of metal present in unknown nutrients or solutions. Colonies must be grown on a very carefully prepared medium which supplies everything necessary for good growth except even the minutest amounts of the metal under investigation. Small amounts of the unknown material will then promote spore production directly in proportion to its metal content. Such a method of **microbiological assay** is often easier than a chemical method for determining very small amounts of metals and has been widely used. Moreover it has a practical advantage in measuring only the metal in an available form. Vitamins may also be assayed in a similar manner by the use of strains of fungi requiring them in external supply.

Physical factors such as temperature, humidity of the atmosphere above the culture and pH of the medium also affect spore production. Vegetative growth is usually possible under a wider range of conditions than will allow sporulation, though cumulative effects of variations are complex. If conditions are favourable enough to allow spore production to start, a change to unfavourable conditions may not prevent the completion of spore formation even though under these changed conditions it could not begin.

The higher Basidiomycetes require special nutritional and climatic conditions before their fruiting bodies are formed, so that we see them in abundance only in autumn, and some appear only at intervals of many years, though the mycelia to which they belong are presumed to persist perennially in the soil. Only a few Basidiomycetes, mainly coprophilous species (growing on dung), can be induced to fruit normally in pure culture which they do readily. What stimulates the others to differentiate is still not known, though their mycelial growths can be cultured easily.

Thick-walled fungal spores, like bacterial endospores, are resistant structures with a low water content, which may remain dormant for long periods withstanding considerable heat, cold and drought, but thin-walled fungal spores are usually short-lived. With the necessary moisture, a suitable temperature and in the absence of toxins or poisons most spores will germinate by swelling and pushing out a narrow **germ tube** which grows into a short hypha using the food reserve of the spore (Fig. 3.3). Most basidiospores as well as some others have small thin areas, called **germ pores**, on the spore wall. It is through these that the first narrow germ . tube appears. If further suitable nutrients are present growth continues, but in the absence of food or with any other sufficiently unfavourable conditions death follows.

NUTRITION

Bacteria and fungi, like other living organisms, require food for liberation of energy and for synthesis of cellular materials. The **heterotrophs** which include all fungi and most bacteria use ready-made organic compounds, usually carbohydrates, as a source of energy. Beyond this basic similarity they show enormous diversity. Some are restricted to one kind of substrate and must have a particular selection of substances to support growth. Those with specific needs may only require, in addition to simple carbohydrates, some mineral salts; others, which are specialized parasites, will grow only on the living cytoplasm of one particular species or variety of plant and, presumably, require all cell compounds ready-made. These *obligate parasites* cannot be cultured on synthetic media or other non-living material. Those saprophytes (p. 82) which normally live in a very rich organic medium may also require many cell compounds ready-made. At

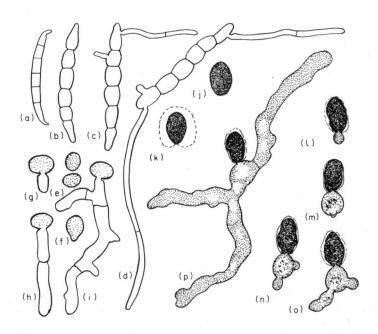

Fig. 3.3 Germination of fungus spores. (a–d) *Fusarium lateritium* : (a) sickle-shaped septate conidium ; (b) same after soaking in distilled water ; (c and d) stages in germination : germ tubes emerging from any cell of the spore ; note constriction at point of emergence. (e–i) *Botrytis cinerea* : (e) ungerminated conidia ; (f) conidium swollen through uptake of water ; (g–i) stages in germination. (j–p) *Sordaria fimicola* : (j) dry ascospore ; (k) ascospore with gelatinous sheath ; (l) early stage in germination, contents extruding into a small vesicle, spore shrinking ; (m–p) later stages in germination showing original vesicle giving rise to hyphae. (After Hawker, L. E. a–i : 1950, *Physiology of Fungi*, University of London Press, London ; j–p : 1951, *Trans. Br. mycol. Soc.*, **34**, 181.)

different stages of growth of an individual organism the nutritional requirements may not be the same, as previously mentioned (p. 52).

Many fungal and bacterial heterotrophs are able to synthesize most of
their requirements, but are unable to make one or more special compounds
such as certain amino acids or vitamins. These organisms with exact
nutritional requirements because of limited synthetic ability are useful as
research tools. If they are grown on a basic medium lacking one necessity
and are then supplied with a series of compounds related to the missing
one they may be able to utilize certain of these in a way which explains or
suggests the metabolic function of the substance, or indicates stages of
its synthesis.

Many other fungal and bacterial heterotrophs have quite unspecialized
or indefinite nutritional requirements and grow well on a great variety of
substrates. The less specialized parasites, including among many others
Botrytis cinerea, *Pythium* spp. and *Pectobacterium* spp., attack a wide range
of plants and usually grow well either on the living organism or on its dead
remains. These organisms can be cultivated easily on various artificial
media. Such fungi and bacteria commonly produce abundant extracellular
enzymes which act first of all on the pectic middle lamellae of plant cell
walls causing plant tissue to dissolve into a mush. Later other carbohydrates and the proteins of the disorganized host cells may be digested
and then the soluble products pass into the hyphae or cells of the parasite
where they are recombined to make the characteristic compounds of the
heterotrophic organism.

Autotrophic bacteria

These are few in number but great in interest. They are able to live in a
completely inorganic medium, obtaining energy either from light, ***photosynthetic autotrophs,*** or from a chemical oxidation, ***chemosynthetic
autotrophs.*** They utilize carbon dioxide to build up carbohydrates and
hence other organic substances. Some organisms which are normally autotrophs have the ability to use organic substances if they are present and so
are ***facultative heterotrophs,*** but others are ***strict autotrophs,*** unable
to use anything but simple inorganic compounds as nutrients, and tied
specifically to one energy source. Examples of strict ***chemosynthetic
autotrophs*** include *Nitrosomonas* which oxidizes ammonium to nitrite so
obtaining energy. The reaction which it promotes is:

$$NH_4^+ \rightarrow NO_2^-$$

Nitrobacter depends exclusively on the oxidation of nitrite to nitrate:

$$NO_2^- \rightarrow NO_3^-$$

Thiobacillus, another chemosynthetic autotroph, depends on the oxidation of sulphur to sulphate:

$$S \rightarrow SO_4^{--}$$

Other sulphur bacteria oxidize hydrogen sulphide and other sulphides, sulphur and thiosulphates. All these autotrophic chemosynthetic bacteria have extremely interesting synthetic abilities. The nitro-bacteria are very important in soil. Each kind is bound strictly to the one energy-yielding reaction, and based on this and utilizing carbon dioxide it will synthesize all cell compounds. Those heterotrophic fungi which, given a simple energy source such as glucose, will then grow on a purely mineral medium have somewhat similar synthesizing systems, but of course lack the ability to fix carbon dioxide freely. The strictly autotrophic bacteria which build carbohydrate from carbon dioxide store food in the cell as glycogen or other polymers, in the same manner as many heterotrophs. They use this stored carbohydrate later in respiration or growth, so that all must have intracellular mechanisms for utilizing carbohydate even though they are not able to assimilate it as the heterotrophs do.

The **photosynthetic bacteria** although ecologically unimportant carry out interesting processes. Their photosynthesis differs in one important detail from that carried out by the normal green plants, though the principle of the reaction is the same. The bacteria contain **bacterio-chlorophyll**, a green pigment with minor differences of structure from higher plant chlorophyll. In members of two groups of these bacteria red and brown pigments are also present making the cells appear purple. By means of these pigments they absorb light energy which enables them to dehydrogenate certain compounds which thus become oxidized. They are unable to obtain hydrogen from water and so never produce oxygen as the green plants do, but instead produce some oxidized by-product from which the hydrogen has been removed. At the same time light energy enables them to build ATP from ADP and phosphate. The hydrogen carried on reduced NAD or NADP and the energy of ATP is then used by the bacteria for the fixation of carbon dioxide and synthesis of carbohydrate. As far as is known the steps in this process are the same as those in the green plant (Fig. 3.4). Carbon dioxide is fixed by combination with ribulosediphosphate, then a complex series of reactions follows in which fructose is formed and ribulosephosphate regenerated, as indicated below.

1. ribulosediphosphate + CO_2 → six-carbon intermediate.
2. six-carbon intermediate immediately → 2 phosphoglyceric acid molecules.
3. phosphoglyceric acid + ATP → diphosphoglyceric acid + ADP.
4. diphosphoglyceric acid + $NADPH_2$ → glyceraldehyde-3-phosphate + H_2O + phosphate + NADP

5. 2 glyceraldehyde-3-phosphate → fructose-1-6-diphosphate.
6. fructose-1-6-diphosphate → fructose-6-phosphate + phosphate.
7. fructose-6-phosphate + glyceraldehyde-3-phosphate [from (5)] → xylulose-5-phosphate (or ribulose-5-phosphate) + erythrose-4-phosphate.
8. erythrose-4-phosphate + fructose-6-phosphate → 2 ribulose-5-phosphate (through sedoheptulose-7-phosphate and glyceraldehyde-3-phosphate).

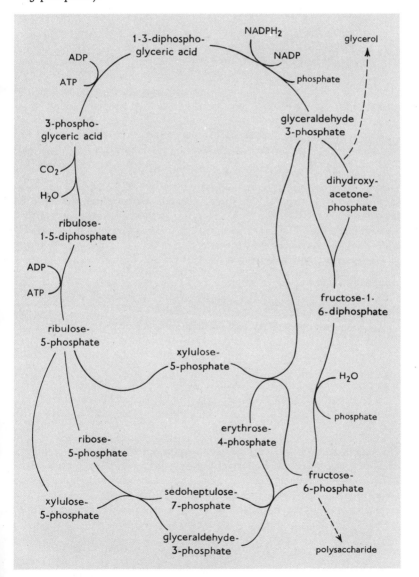

Fig. 3.4 Cycle of reactions in photosynthetic CO_2 fixation.

The three distinct groups of photosynthetic bacteria are:

1 *Green sulphur bacteria*: Chlorobacteriaceae. All species of this group are strictly autotrophic anaerobes which grow in a purely mineral medium using hydrogen from hydrogen sulphide or other sulphur compounds.

2 *Purple sulphur bacteria*: Thiorhodaceae. These are mostly strictly autotrophic anaerobes which use hydrogen sulphide or other sulphur compounds as a source of hydrogen, though a few may use molecular hydrogen. They grow in a purely inorganic medium but under certain conditions some species may use organic acids as a source of hydrogen instead of reduced sulphur compounds.

3 *Purple non-sulphur bacteria*: Athiorhodaceae. The members of this family are photosynthetic organisms which are not strictly autotrophic as they require various organic compounds as a source of hydrogen, and also need organic growth substances which they normally obtain from the organic mud in pools where they live. They grow anaerobically in light, fixing carbon dioxide, and under the same conditions many also readily fix nitrogen. Some are able to grow heterotrophically and aerobically in the dark.

Apart from its utilization in photosynthesis carbon dioxide is also necessary for many fungi and bacteria which grow heterotrophically (p. 38). As far as is known all carbon dioxide fixation involves combination with a preformed carbon chain. Carbon dioxide is used as a hydrogen acceptor by certain organisms which thus produce formic acid or methane.

The elements which·fungi and bacteria require for their nutrition are:

hydrogen and oxygen as water;
oxygen as gas for aerobes;
hydrogen as gas for a few anaerobic bacteria;
carbon as carbon dioxide, carbohydrate or other organic compound;
nitrogen as ammonium, nitrate, nitrite, amino acid, organic base, or as gas for nitrogen-fixing organisms (p. 70);
phosphorus as phosphate;
sulphur as the element, sulphate or other sulphur compound;
magnesium, calcium, potassium and iron in very small amounts;
manganese, zinc, copper, cobalt, molybdenum, and possibly a few other metals, in traces only.

Vitamins are required by some heterotrophs though it is only compounds of the B group which are important. So far as is known vitamin A (carotene compounds), vitamin C (ascorbic acid) and vitamin D (ergosterol), which are all important to higher animals and some higher plants, are not required in external supply by fungi and bacteria. A recently-discovered vitamin, α-lipoic acid, is needed by some bacteria under certain conditions. It has been found that this compound catalyses the formation of acetate from pyruvic acid. A few other similar special requirements are known. Under some culture conditions certain micro-organisms produce much more of some vitamins than they need, a situation which is put to commercial use in the preparation of extracts of riboflavin from certain yeasts and cyanocobalamin (vitamin B_{12}) from some actinomycetes or bacteria (p. 117).

Toxins or Poisons

The harmful effect of many bacteria causing disease in animals is due to production of toxins. These may be *endotoxins* formed in the cells and released when they die and disintegrate, or they may be *exotoxins* which are secreted by the cells, and which may be compounds of almost incredible virulence. The exotoxin of *Clostridium botulinum* is fatal to a white mouse in a dose of 5×10^{-5} μg. Most toxins are unstable compounds, but a few are stable. All bacterial toxins so far analysed are proteins. Some, possibly all, are the protein part of an important cell enzyme, such as a respiratory enzyme without its prosthetic group. When such toxic substances enter susceptible living organisms they disorganize the corresponding enzyme system. The small amount of toxin which is effective indicates the small amount of an important enzyme which may be present in an organism. The most powerful bacterial toxins act on the nervous system while other serious toxins cause lysis, or breakdown and solution, of blood cells.

Many fungi also contain poisons and if eaten by people or possibly other mammals can prove fatal. Some small animals such as slugs seem to be able to eat them with impunity. The most deadly and dangerous fungus is the agaric *Amanita phalloides*, a small piece of which contains enough poison to spell certain death to a human being. The dangerous compounds which it contains are found also in some other *Amanita* spp. They act on the liver and then on the central nervous system. *Pithomyces chartarum* produces a powerful liver toxin (p. 101). Ergot, *Claviceps purpurea* (Fig. 3.5), contains several very poisonous compounds which may cause serious disease or death. Convulsions, paralysis and hallucinations follow if it is eaten, the condition formerly being called St. Anthony's Fire. Small controlled doses of ergot, as of some other poisons, have uses in medicine. Both *A. muscaria* and *Panaeolus sphinctrinus* are toadstools producing hallucinatory compounds, which native peoples have used as intoxicants, but prolonged use has damaging effects. Fungi in culture frequently produce poisons and other biologically active compounds of varying potency which may affect the growth of the fungi that produce them, or that of other organisms. These substances range from staling compounds to useful antibiotics. Toxins or poisons are not known to play any part in the

3*

metabolism of the organisms which form them and may simply be waste products.

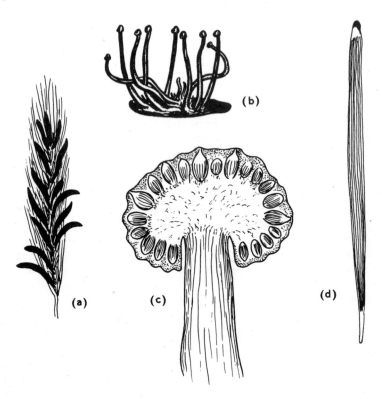

Fig. 3.5 Ergot of rye : (a) sclerotia in ripe ear ($\times\frac{1}{3}$) ; (b) stromata growing from sclerotium ($\times 1\frac{1}{3}$) ; (c) section of head of stroma showing perithecia ($\times 45$) ; (d) single ascus with 8 filiform ascospores, each 100 μ long ($\times 660$).

PART II

SPECIAL HABITATS AND ECONOMIC ASPECTS

4

Soil, Air and Water

SOIL

The vegetation of the earth's surface is dependent on the thin coat of soil, usually a few feet thick, which lies over the rock crust. The soil itself is often called 'the living soil', because the living organisms within it are one of its major components, and also because the whole complex mixture which makes up its mass is in a continuous state of flux, being worn away and eaten up while it is growing and developing. In order that the fungi and bacteria of the soil may be seen in perspective with their environment, which to a large extent they control, and from which they can scarcely be separated, a general account of soil is given below in outline.

Composition

Soil consists of:

1. particles of mineral matter;
2. particles of dead organic matter;
3. living micro-organisms;
4. soil solution forming a surface film over these solids;
5. soil atmosphere filling all spaces.

The *mineral fragments* are derived usually from the underlying rocks by physical and chemical weathering, but are sometimes carried from a distance by wind or water. They consist of different chemical compounds, mostly complex silicates, which vary in composition according to the type of parent rock. They vary also in physical form from grains of sand, through smaller particles of silt to submicroscopic colloidal flakes of clay. The physical properties of the soil are largely influenced by the proportions of different sized mineral grains. A sandy soil is open, dry and warm. A good loam contains mainly silt. Clay alone is cold, wet and sticky, very retentive of water and mineral salts. A proportion of each kind of mineral fragment can confer its own advantages on a soil mixture.

The *dead organic fraction* consists of the remains of animals and, more abundantly, the waste material of the plant and microbial life which the soil supports. Dead material freshly contributed and all stages of its decomposition are present. Fine roots are being sloughed off within the soil by plants as they grow, and leaves and branches are continually dying and being added to the surface as **litter**. The living organisms of soil consist mainly of a multitude of bacteria and fungi, many of them short-lived, which grow on the organic wastes to which they also contribute when they die. The early stages in breaking down cellulose tissues of dead plants are readily accomplished by many fungi and also by some cellulose-digesting bacteria. The later stages of decomposition, which result finally in the formation of humus, appear to depend more on the activities of bacteria.

Humus, which is the most important part of the dead organic matter, is a residual material left when most of the organic waste has been consumed by microbial growth. It is not a single readily identifiable compound, but consists of a complex of substances the proportions of which vary according to where and how the soil has been formed. Humus is always a dark brown, sticky colloidal mixture, with no trace of anatomical structure of any of the tissues or cells from which it is derived. It holds water and prevents soil from drying out. It is extremely important in sticking the mineral particles together to form the crumbs which give the soil a definite structure, so allowing good aeration and drainage and thus favouring growth of both higher plants and micro-organisms. The binding effect may be due in part to fungal hyphae and to the slime of bacteria living in the humus. Some soil bacteria grow in the humus slowly destroying it, but it is not readily degraded by micro-organisms. As long as organic matter is being added to soil, and micro-organisms are active, more humus is being formed. If the normal balance is destroyed by over-cultivation or insufficient manuring, humus will gradually disappear; then the soil loses its structure, a calamity which is difficult to repair. It is easy nowadays to add chemical fertilizers to the soil to stimulate plant growth, but it is very important for agriculture that the soil organic matter is maintained for the sake of structure and for biological activity within the soil.

Composition of humus

The humus mixture of compounds contains about 10 per cent of nitrogen which can be recovered as amino acids. These obviously are not present in humus in the form of protein which is a class of compound always destroyed with great rapidity if it is added to soil. The amino acids appear to be combined in some way with a lignin residue from decomposed plant skeletal tissue. The lignins are stable cyclic carbon compounds remaining when the cellulose of xylem and fibre has been digested. They vary in composition according to the plant from which they are derived, but are always stable phenylpropane compounds, which contain from 1 to 3 per cent of nitrogen. About 10 per cent of the humus consists of various polysaccharides such as polyuronides. An important fraction of humus is formed of humic acids, organic acids the exact composition of which is undetermined. A certain amount of phosphorus and sulphur also forms part of these various complex humus substances. The slow breakdown of humus releases nitrogen, phosphorus and sulphur which become available to plant roots, and in this way the humus acts as a reservoir of nutrients.

The **soil solution** is derived from rain falling directly on the surface and also from water draining from adjacent land. As it flows over and between the solid particles it dissolves mineral salts and also, especially from the litter, it collects carbon dioxide, organic acids and other compounds which are produced there by the micro-organisms. The dissolved acids increase the amounts of mineral salts that the soil water can carry.

The **soil atmosphere** is much affected by the movement of soil water because the atmosphere occupies all spaces not filled by soil solution. When rain runs into the soil some of the atmosphere is forced out, but when the soil drains or dries again fresh air is drawn in. The respiration of plant roots and soil organisms adds carbon dioxide to the soil atmosphere. Some is taken into solution by the soil water, but the soil atmosphere normally has a higher carbon dioxide content than free air. The oxygen content of the uppermost layers may be that of the normal atmosphere, but at greater depths in the soil, depending on texture and conditions, it is usually lower especially close to roots or growing hyphae. Anaerobic bacteria exist in the lower subsoil where oxygen must be lacking.

Soil profile

An old well-developed soil shows a distinct stratification into horizons which can be seen clearly in profile on the sides of any cutting through the surface strata. A newly formed or rapidly developing soil, such as that on a steep slope where there is some continuous movement, will show little or no separation into layers, the result being what is called a skeletal soil. Where rainfall is considerable soluble salts are leached out of the topsoil and carried to lower strata or even removed completely in water draining away into rivers. Clay particles are also sufficiently small and light to be carried with soil water, and so tend to be removed from topsoil and to accumulate in subsoil. This action of water contributes to the development of stratification. Other factors involved are the amount of weathering of the rock fragments—which is greatest in the upper layers where micro-organisms are most active and where temperature changes and drying and rewetting are most frequent—and, also, the superficial deposition of dead tissue.

The top or litter layer formed from the organic material collecting on the surface is called the A_0 horizon. The highly weathered topsoil which contains most of the organic matter and soil micro-organisms is called the A_1 horizon. The B horizon is the less weathered, mainly mineral, subsoil which may contain material washed or leached from the A_1. The C horizon is a slightly weathered zone grading into parent rock (Fig. 4.1).

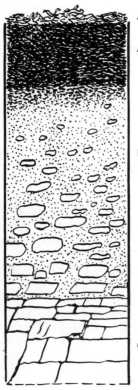

A_0 litter layer of raw humus with many specific fungi and bacteria.

A_1 Topsoil with much decomposing organic matter, very large numbers of micro-organisms, a reservoir of humus, and well-weathered mineral matter.

B   subsoil with little organic matter, finely divided mineral matter including clay particles, and coarse unweathered rock fragments; few micro-organisms.

C   parent rock breaking at surface to give loose fragments.

Fig. 4.1 Diagram of horizons in a soil profile.

Soil formation

The factors which control the formation of soil are interacting. They are: climate; biotic factors, including firstly vegetation and micro-organisms, and secondly human and animal interference; lastly, and usually of less importance, parent rock and topography. Each of the major climatic zones has its own general soil type associated with a characteristic vegetation. These zonal soil types are outlined in Table 4.1. Within these broad,

Table 4.1 Zonal Soil Types

Soil	Climate	Vegetation	Appearance and agriculture
tundra	arctic	tundra vegetation	peat overlying blue-grey mineral soil : not used
podzol	cold temperate	coniferous forest	raw humus or *mor* over a bleached layer, brown subsoil : made by and used for coniferous forest
brown earth	warm temperate	deciduous forest	*mull* merging into brown topsoil which grades into subsoil : suited to careful cultivation
chernozem or black earth	hot, dry summer cold, wet winter	grassland	very deep, rich soil : ideal for agriculture
red earth	tropical	tropical	leached and oxidized soils high in iron : difficult for agriculture

generalized divisions there are many sub-divisions, so that the soil of each country or land mass is a mosaic of different specific types.

The most obvious indication of what a soil is like is the vegetation which may be seen growing on it, and which returns its own special kind of organic debris. This in turn supports a definite community of micro-organisms which by their activities help to form the soil. The macro-vegetation with its mycorrhizal fungi and the micro-organisms of the litter, including thousands of species of agarics, are inseparable partners in each type of soil, though the fungi and bacteria of the topsoil include many that are cosmopolitan.

Zonal types

Tundra soil

Under sub-arctic or sub-antarctic conditions where plants grow very slowly micro-organisms act even more slowly. Plant remains accumulate as peat, a partially decomposed material also known as raw humus. Under temperate conditions where soil is waterlogged plant remains also form peat. Oxygen is deficient below the surface and the slow fungal growths possible under these conditions produce acids which still further reduce microbial activity and hinder decomposition. In a few places under arctic and antarctic conditions a true soil is found consisting of mineral detritus supporting minimal biological activity (Plate 6A).

Podzol formation

In cold-temperate regions where needle-leaved trees flourish, rainfall is high while evaporation is low. Soluble salts are readily washed out of surface layers. The pines or other vegetation absorb only very small amounts of bases from the soil, so the litter which they return to the surface layers is poor in bases and forms a *mor*. This accumulates as a tough, fibrous, litter layer which supports the growth of fungi, but is on the whole too acid for bacteria. Rain washing through this acid litter also becomes acidified, due to traces of oxalic and citric acids, as well as humic acids, produced by the litter fungi. The acidified percolating water then has a strong leaching action on the upper layer of soil, which is impoverished and bleached to an ash colour. The Russians, who are very active in soil science, call this formation a podzol, meaning an ash-soil. The pale, ash-coloured layer is very sharply demarcated from the litter layer above it, and also from the subsoil which is typically brown. Such a soil made by the coniferous vegetation can support only this type of vegetation (Plate 6B).

Under conditions of heavy rainfall, particularly where temperatures are moderate, the leaching beneath pine forests is intensified. Both iron and humus are rapidly removed from the topsoil by the acidified percolating water, but they may be deposited again as a solid layer or pan between the topsoil and the less acid subsoil. The growth of iron bacteria under anaerobic conditions, caused by a high water table, may also contribute to the precipitation of the iron. Such a soil with an *iron pan* cannot be drained and supports only a bog vegetation. The pines have then ruined the soil even for themselves and a bog may follow in succession to the forest.

Brown earth formation

Deciduous or other broad-leaved forest, in comparison with coniferous, makes greater demands on the mineral soil from which it takes up a good supply of mineral salts, especially of basic ions. Rainfall, though considerable, is sufficiently moderate to leave an adequate supply of nutrients in the soil. The litter which this type of forest returns to the surface is thus better supplied with mineral salts and bases, and forms a fertile *mull*, a friable, brown leaf-mould which supports vigorous growth of both fungi and bacteria. It breaks down rapidly into humus materials which are soon incorporated into the topsoil, both by the activity of the worms that are encouraged by this formation, and also by the washing action of the rain. There is no sharp boundary between topsoil and subsoil but the A_1 horizon grades from very dark brown at the surface, to less darkly coloured below, where it fades into the paler B horizon. Valuable mineral salts are taken from the subsoil by this vegetation and returned to the topsoil, so that the fertility of the forest is maintained. If the land is cleared the soil is reasonably fertile, although without careful management the high rainfall of the forest zone may lead to leaching (Plate 6C).

Chernozem or black earth

A grass vegetation and a moderate rainfall result in a great development of humus. The fine fibrous roots of grasses penetrate the mineral soil to considerable depths and are frequently renewed, so that a great deal of organic matter is added to the soil throughout its depth. It has been estimated that grass roots in such a community add over a ton of dry matter per acre to soil in a year. Fine dead leaves and droppings from grazing animals enrich the surface. The low rainfall of steppe regions does not leach the soil, so that soluble salts accumulate in the top layer and are available to support further vigorous plant growth. Under these conditions soil bacteria are very active though fungi are also present. Humus increases and a great depth of fertile soil may build up, such as the famous black earths of eastern Europe, the Russian steppes and the American prairies (Plate 6D).

Soil microflora

The topsoil houses a vast population of interacting and interdependent micro-organisms which are most numerous around living roots in the region called the **rhizosphere**. Numbers fluctuate enormously, but true bacteria are the most abundant, amounting to roughly from 50 to 5,000 millions per gram. The Actinomycetes or filamentous bacteria are the next most important, then follow the fungi and the Myxomycetes. Though many fewer in numbers of species or individuals, the fungi have about the same mass as the bacteria. Algae and protozoa may also be fairly numerous, but appear to be less important. The most fertile soils usually contain the greatest numbers of micro-organisms. Bacteria generally flourish in neutral to alkaline soils, while fungi are usually favoured by acid conditions. It is probable that soil contains organisms capable of decomposing every known kind of organic substance, otherwise resistant compounds would have accumulated long ago. Under special circumstances peat and coal collect and form deposits but strong drugs, disinfectants and some normally durable materials such as plastics disappear when buried in soil.

Even more important is the fact that soil organisms are able to decompose effectively almost all of the great range of hormones, antibiotics, insecticides and weedkillers used in modern agriculture, whose survival, if prolonged, would have disastrous effects. It is extremely important that no substances too resistant to be broken down in soil should be used in agriculture, and for this reason new compounds must be carefully examined before they are put on the market.

Carbon and mineral salts cycle

The dead plant material, which is the principal addition to soil, consists mainly of carbohydrate and has a high C/N ratio. It is attacked by cellulose digesting fungi and bacteria which oxidize most of the carbohydrate rapidly to water and carbon dioxide. This gas returns directly to the atmosphere, with a consequent progressive decrease in the C/N ratio of the residue. Humus, the end product, has a low C/N ratio, about 10:1, compared with fresh plant substance which has a ratio of about 100:1. The rate of decomposition of fresh plant residues is always stimulated by adding nitrogen compounds. The elements phosphorus and sulphur locked up in organic compounds in living organisms are released back to the soil as phosphate and sulphate during their decay. Metals such as calcium, potassium, magnesium, and many others, together with the radicals phosphate and sulphate, cycle directly in this way. They are taken up by plants from soil and incorporated into organic compounds, then returned again in the litter. Subsequently they are released by the microbial digestion of the cell material and washed back into the topsoil whence they came.

Nitrogen cycle

Of all the elements in the chemical compounds which plants absorb from the soil, nitrogen is required in greatest quantity and has the biggest effect on growth (Fig. 4.2). Within the soil it undergoes the most variable transformations. The fertility of soil is generally proportional to its nitrogen content as well as to microbial numbers, and nitrogenous fertilizers give the most conspicuous crop stimulation. Although the atmosphere is four-fifths nitrogen, little of this is ever absorbed into vegetable substance. The higher plants take up their nitrogen mostly as nitrates—and to a lesser extent as ammonium compounds—from the soil. When nitrogen is absorbed as nitrate it has to be reduced to ammonium before it can be used for amino acid, and then protein, synthesis. When the dead cell material is returned to the soil the protein is quickly digested by saprophytes which absorb some of the nitrogen into their own cells, but which also liberate

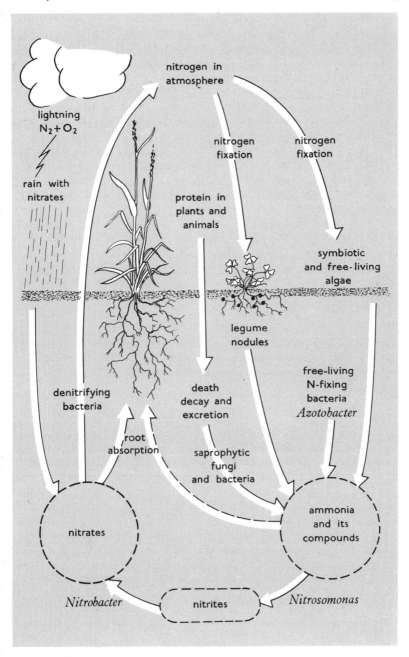

Fig. 4.2 Diagram illustrating nitrogen cycle in nature.

quantities of ammonia into the soil. If this is directly reabsorbed by plants a short cycle is completed, but in fact little follows this pathway. The ammonia is very soluble, moves quickly in the soil and is rapidly acted on by micro-organisms. It is used up almost as quickly as it is formed, so that only the merest traces are ever detected in soil.

A chain of chemosynthetic autotrophs (p. 55) which oxidize ammonia occur commonly in soil. Firstly, *Nitrosomonas* oxidizes ammonia to nitrite. Then as quickly as the nitrite is formed *Nitrobacter* oxidizes it to nitrate. These two kinds of organisms derive their energy from these oxidations and use bicarbonate ions as a basis for carbohydrate synthesis. Both are common in soil and this process of formation of nitrate, which is called **nitrification**, is going on continuously, following the liberation of ammonia by soil saprophytes from fresh organic wastes, or from the humus reservoir.

The opposite process of nitrate reduction is carried out by all organisms which absorb nitrate and incorporate this nitrogen, as ammonia, into their cell protein, but many soil organisms, especially under conditions of intense microbial activity where soil is richly manured, use nitrate as a hydrogen acceptor and liberate nitrogen gas, or occasionally nitrous oxide. The bacteria which use nitrate in this way are indifferent organisms (p. 36) which are active under both aerobic and anaerobic conditions. Considerable amounts of molecular nitrogen are thus released from soil, the process being called **denitrification**. Losses amount to an average of about 20 lb of nitrogen per acre per year, and may occur both in poorly-aerated soil with low microbiological activity and in well-aerated soil where microbial action is stimulated.

Nitrogen gains

If the soil maintains its fertility the very considerable losses of nitrogen from denitrification, and through drainage, must be balanced by more or less equal gains. Under natural conditions, in fact, most soils gradually improve and gain nitrogen. Electrical discharges in the atmosphere bring about the formation of traces of nitrogen compounds so that rain-water carries down small amounts of ammonia and nitrates, which may amount to a total addition of from 1 to 5 lb per acre per year. The largest additions to soil nitrogen come from the biological fixation process, by which atmospheric nitrogen is converted directly in the living cells into organic nitrogen compounds. This occurs mainly in symbiotic root nodules, but small amounts are also added by the activities of free-living micro-organisms.

Symbiotic nitrogen fixation

Many species of legumes (Leguminosae) and a few others such as alder, *Alnus glutinosa*, bog myrtle, *Myrica gale*, and species of the genera *Coriaria*,

Elaeagnus, Ceanothus and *Casuarina*, have nitrogen-fixing root nodules which contain a dense mass of symbiotic micro-organisms. In leguminous plants the symbiont is a bacterium of the genus *Rhizobium*, of which there are a number of strains each restricted to a few closely-related plants (Fig. 4.3a). In alder and the other non-leguminous plants mentioned the symbiont appears to be a member of the Plasmodiophorales but, as it has not yet been possible to isolate and culture the organism, its exact identity remains in doubt. Some other plants such as the water fern *Azolla* and species of *Gunnera* (Haloragaceae) have nitrogen-fixing symbionts which are blue-green algae. Some tropical plants such as *Pavetta indica* and other species have bacterial nodules on the leaves, which may also fix nitrogen (Fig. 4.3b). It is mainly the legumes, especially the clovers, which are of

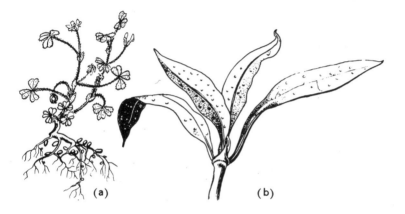

Fig. 4.3   (a) Part of a well-nodulated *Trifolium subterraneum* plant ($\times\frac{1}{2}$). (b) Leaves of *Pavetta indica* with nodules ($\times\frac{1}{2}$).

practical importance, and they have been used in agriculture since the earliest times to improve soil. In Great Britain they are valuable in pasture, especially on hill country where it is not easy to apply nitrogenous fertilizers. They are very important in countries such as Australia and New Zealand, and even in southern Europe wherever climatic conditions are favourable for legumes.

Development of legume nodules

Where suitable strains of bacteria are not present in the soil they must be introduced, but when once established they seem to remain in the soil indefinitely. Roots of leguminous plants secrete substances which attract the bacteria on to their surfaces, where the bacteria in turn secrete a substance, probably a growth hormone, which causes some of the root hairs to curl. The bacteria have been seen to penetrate the curled root hair cell through which they grow in a continuous thread-like mass, till they reach the cortex of the root. Here they fill many cells with a dense mass of swollen, or Y-shaped, abnormal bacteria called bacteroids, in spite of which the living protoplast of each invaded parenchyma cell is neither damaged nor killed, but is rather stimulated and has a specially conspicuous nucleus. The cortical cells around the early infection are stimulated to divide and grow to form an enlarged nodule, somewhat like a short, thick branch root, with a definite structure. A central mass of tissue containing bacteroids is surrounded by a bacteria-free cortical zone a few cell layers thick. There is a meristematic region at the apex while the base is supplied with a branch vascular strand (Fig. 4.4).

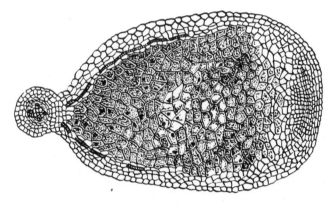

Fig. 4.4 Diagram of a section of a legume nodule showing meristematic tip, uninfected cortex, vascular strands and central mass of enlarged cells full of bacteroids (× c.60).

The centre of an active nodule is red, due to formation of a haemoglobin which, like the nitrogen fixation, results from the symbiosis (p. 83). As the nodule grows, part of the nitrogen fixed passes into the tissues of the legume and part passes out into the surrounding soil where it stimulates the growth of plants associated with the legume. Neither bacterium nor root alone can fix nitrogen or produce haemoglobin.

If the roots should become invaded by an ineffective strain of *Rhizobium* very small nodules are formed in which no haemoglobin develops and no nitrogen is fixed. In a good pasture composed of white clover and ryegrass in New Zealand the legume nodules fix about 700 lb of nitrogen per acre per year. This is the main basis for the fertility of the high-production dairy farms. In Great Britain, where the climate is less favourable, the highest rate of fixation seems to be about half this figure, and usually it is lower. Nevertheless it may amount to a substantial gain in soil nitrogen. If a grass-clover ley is used in a crop rotation, as is the practice in many parts, the soil is usefully enriched by the nitrogen fixed in the legume nodules.

Free-living nitrogen-fixing bacteria

These are *Azotobacter*, *Beijerinckia* and related organisms which are aerobic, and *Clostridium* and a few other anaerobic organisms. As plant roots do not normally penetrate to anaerobic depths in the soil any nitrogen fixed and released by *Clostridium* is likely to be lost in drainage water. *Azotobacter* has proved a very useful laboratory organism for experiments on nitrogen fixation, and for examining the pathways followed during the process. Under natural conditions this aerobic nitrogen-fixing bacterium occurs in fertile soils where supplies of nitrogen are already sufficient for plant growth at a level known to suppress nitrogen fixation by *Azotobacter*. These organisms appear to live in fertile soils mainly as very active saprophytes, but not as nitrogen fixers. The importance of the free-living nitrogen-fixing organisms in natural soils is probably not very great. Although clovers are of great benefit in adding nitrogen to cultivated soils, neither these nor other known nitrogen-fixing plants are found in forests where soil nitrogen builds up steadily. Our knowledge of how soil nitrogen is maintained or increased under natural conditions is still incomplete.

MICROBIOLOGY OF THE AIR

When rays of bright light strike across a dark room the dust of the air can be seen as innumerable bright specks. Though always present they are visible only in such special circumstances. Most of these myriads of minute particles are alive. They include, firstly, spores of all kinds of microorganisms but predominantly those of fungi. Secondly, there are floating bacterial cells and viral particles together with any organic or inorganic fragments to which they may be stuck, and even some algal cells may be present. Lastly, there are microspores of flowering plants, the pollen grains. All these small to minute cells in the air are of characteristic shape and size, which usually allow identification to be made by microscopic examination.

Importance of air-borne spores

The dispersal of the reproductive cells of most kinds of fungi and of many other micro-organisms depends on carriage by air. In the case of many plant pathogens and destructive saprophytes, this has economic consequences so that it is obviously important to know how and when it occurs. Bacteria in the air also may include pathogens, and some of the virus particles may be viable and cause infection if they reach a suitable host. The virus or viruses of common cold are air-borne in this way, and so also are bacteriophages including those which destroy bacterial cultures used as 'starters' in cheese making. This latter kind of air-borne infection has proved very troublesome and even disastrous in some cheese factories.

Certain fungal spores when present in air breathed by people who are allergic cause irritation of varying degrees of intensity which may even result in such illness as hay fever, though this is usually due to pollen. 'Farmer's lung', a complaint suffered by some farm workers after handling mouldy hay, is generally an acute allergic condition, but occasionally actual infection of the lungs may occur. Such allergies are thought to be due to the presence in the cells of specific proteins.

Dispersal, deposition and sampling

The atmosphere often moves actively as wind due to temperature differences between air masses and other physical causes, but even when wind is not obvious there is always a certain amount of air movement. Within enclosed buildings temperature differences are normally sufficient to result in active air currents. This turbulence suffices to distribute dust and to keep some or most of it in suspension. If air is enclosed in a sealed glass box, it may be shown, by shining a light through it periodically, that the dust gradually settles. All the cells and other particles are heavier than air, but their very small size, and therefore their large surface-area-to-volume ratio, allows them to float in air currents. The pollen grains and many of the spores are more or less spherical, ranging commonly from about 5 to 25 μ in diameter. Other spores and inert particles may be long and narrow, or flattened, and so float even more easily. A range of spore size and shape is indicated in Fig. 4.5.

From moving air some cells sink and are deposited on the surfaces over which the air flows. At the same time new spores may be swept up by the air stream. Spores may be blown against objects and impacted on to them most easily when they are of large size. Rain very effectively washes spores out of the air, so that immediately after a brief period of rain the air may be relatively clean. However, rain and moisture on vegetation and litter encourage the growth of fungi, especially in warm weather, and so stimulate a new supply of spores. Many fungal fructifications, such as Basidiomycete puff-balls and especially sporophores of many Ascomycetes, may be stimulated by rain to discharge spores already formed.

Samples of air-borne spores may be collected by exposing a sticky microscope slide to an enclosed volume of air from which the cells settle out. More usually, a large measured volume of air is allowed to flow over

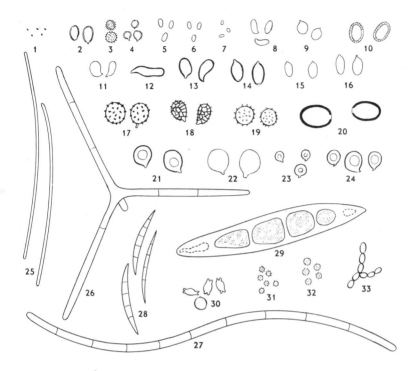

Fig. 4.5 Range of spore size and shape: 1 bacterial endospores; 2 *Crucibulum vulgare*; 3 *Lycoperdon pyriforme*; 4 *Calvatia gigantea*; 5 *Ileodictyon cibarius*; 6 *Aseroe rubra* ; 7 *Phallus impudicus* ; 8 *Stereum purpureum* ; 9 *Sparassis crispa* ; 10 *Ganoderma applanatum*; 11 *Phaeolus schweinitzii*; 12 *Boletus edulis*; 13 *Cantharellus cibarius* ; 14 *Coprinus lagopus* ; 15 *Agaricus campestris* ; 16 *Paxillus involutus* ; 17 *Russula emetica* ; 18 *Lactarius deliciosus* ; 19 *Laccaria laccata* ; 20 *Lepiota procera* ; 21 *Amanita phalloides* ; 22 *A. muscaria* ; 23 *Clavaria fusiformis* ; 24 *C. cinerea* ; 25 *Flagellospora curvula* ; 26 *Lemonniera aquatica* ; 27 *Anguillospora longissima* ; 28 *Fusarium* sp. ; 29 *Helminthosporium monoceras* ; 30 biconvex, grooved ascospores of *Eurotium* sp. ; 31 *Aspergillus* sp. ; 32 *Aspergillus* sp. ; 33 chains of *Monilia* conidia (all ×525). (25–27, aquatic fungi, after Ingold, C. T., 1953, *Dispersal in Fungi*, Clarendon Press, Oxford.)

a sticky slide which 'traps' the spores. This method is most effective for particles with a diameter of about 3–40 μ, and so collects the majority of the pollen grains and fungal spores but most bacterial cells escape. Air can be sampled also by bubbling it through a wash bottle in which all the particles collect. If the washings are concentrated by centrifuging or filtration they can be examined directly, or samples from them may be inoculated into culture media in which some of the bacteria and fungi will grow. Pasteur was the first to show the presence of germs in the air when he exposed flasks of sterilized nutrient broth which subsequently developed vigorous growths. Similar flasks protected from air-borne dust remained sterile. Culture methods of sampling spores from the air are laborious and not very satisfactory because different kinds of organisms require different media and different conditions for growth. If the spores of any quickly-developing fungus are present, blanketing growths are likely to smother everything else. Rusts and other obligate parasites will never grow. For routine examinations the direct observation of sticky slides exposed in a spore trap is the widely adopted method, even though it does not distinguish between viable and dead cells. Measurement of air-spora by culture methods has shown that there are approximately twice as many viable bacteria present as there are viable fungal spores.

Origins of air-spora

The wind-borne pollen which is associated with fungal spores and bacteria in the air is of strictly seasonal occurrence. After a burst in spring and early summer it falls to a low level.

The bacterial cells and viral particles which float in the air are thought to be picked up mainly by the wind with dust from the surface of the ground and thus are most abundant near arable land and in cities. Some also come from drying sea spray, and some from coughing and sneezing of man and other animals. They may become launched into the air at any time of the year and remain in circulation for long periods. Ultra-violet radiation readily kills them, and they are washed out by rain, so that air over high mountains and in polar regions contains few or no viable bacteria.

The fungal spores in the air arise largely within the layer of vegetation and litter where innumerable fungi grow. Many of these actively discharge their spores into the air by some mechanism, though others simply expose masses of dry conidia which air currents pick up. The growth of fungi on plants and litter is most active in warm moist weather, but continues with abundant spore production from spring till autumn. During winter few fungal spores are released into the air. The commonest types of air-borne spore are those of *Cladosporium* spp. and of the mirror yeasts which originate mainly from saprophytic growths on moribund grasses.

Whenever crops are attacked by fungi there is likely to be a large production of fungal spores. Areas of grain crops infected with rust or mildews give off clouds of spores, some of which may travel great distances. Rust of wheat travels north in America from Mexico and infects crops as far distant as the Canadian prairies. In northern Europe wheat may become infected by rust spores carried in the air from Portugal or Algeria. In the warmer southern countries grain grows throughout the winter carrying the infection which dies out in the more severe northern winter. Near to infected wheat crops large concentrations of rust fungus spores are carried in the air, and though many settle near by, some reach considerable altitudes and are then carried long distances. Ultra-violet light kills fungal spores as well as bacterial cells, after moderate exposure, and may be used to sterilize air, but coloured or thick-walled spores such as those of the rusts may remain viable in air for considerable periods.

Variations in air-spora

The numbers and kinds of cells in the air vary greatly according to such conditions as locality, season and time of day. The nearness of sporing colonies of particular fungal species is clearly important, or the exposure of dry soil or dry town dust which provide bacteria. In polar regions or on high mountains the air may be almost free from living dust. Cold winters in temperate regions may clear the air but with the return of spring there is a sudden increase in air-borne cells. The systematic trapping of spores is carried on in many places to chart the daily or even hourly changes. Examples of the measure of total spores in the air are given in Table 4.2. An indication of the composition of air-spora is given in Table 4.3.

Table 4.2　Total Spore Content per m^3 of Air Recorded by a Portable Spore Trap 2 m above Ground Level at Rothamsted

Date	Time	Fungal spores	Pollen	Total
26.7.1953	c. 12.00 hrs	13,050	450	13,500
26.7.1953	c. 16.00 hrs	17,700	600	18,300
17.7.1953	c. 12.00 hrs			39,000
29.7.1953	c. 02.00 hrs			18,000

(Adapted from P. H. Gregory, 1954, *Trans. Br. mycol. Soc.*, **37**, 401.)

Table 4.3　Average number of Air-borne Spores per m^3 at Rothamsted, May–September 1954

Pollen grains	122
'Phycomycete' spores	200
Ascospores	3,000
Basidiospores	5,000
Fungi Imperfecti spores	6,000

(Adapted from Elizabeth Hamilton, 1959, *Acta allerg.*, **13**, 143–175.)

It is apparent that the air is an efficient agent for carrying very large numbers of spores, some of which survive long journeys. The total amount of contamination in the air during the growing season may be considerable.

MICROBIOLOGY OF WATER

Water supplies

The quality of water for household and many industrial purposes depends largely on the micro-organisms it carries. Modern standards demand continuous supplies of safe, pure water, which requires local authorities to maintain large water-treatment works. Rain-water is often thought to be pure but, as already shown, it may wash down large numbers of living cells among which pathogens may be represented. However, whenever the rain flows over the surface of the ground into rivers it collects a great many more micro-organisms and also dissolved salts. Such water collected into lakes and reservoirs may support further vigorous growths. Where nutrients accumulate the lakes or reservoirs are called *eutrophic* and produce a rich plankton growth, but in other bodies of water the nutrients remain low and the water supports the growth of many fewer micro-organisms. These lakes are called *oligotrophic*. A year's parallel records of two such contrasting town supply reservoirs are given in Fig. 4.6.

In spring and summer the most conspicuous growths in lakes and reservoirs are the plankton algae which are seasonal and which are restricted to a surface layer 5–10 m thick. A few fungi grow on dying plankton, but most of the water fungi are found on the remains of littoral vegetation. Bacteria are always present throughout the mass of water and in the bottom mud. They convert the organic wastes as they do in soil, and many of the same species are present. In water the processes are more or less complete without the accumulation of any humus residue. Lignin is virtually absent from the organic cycle in water masses. Carbohydrates are broken down to carbon dioxide and water, while nitrogenous compounds are converted first to ammonia, then to nitrates which accumulate to a small extent in winter. Bacterial numbers rise as the plankton disappears. The spring resurgence of plankton algae quickly exhausts the nitrate store and depresses bacterial growth.

Well water collected directly from deep strata is often sterile because all organisms are filtered out of it, but as such water usually has a high concentration of dissolved salts micro-organisms grow in it abundantly when it is exposed to the air. Shallow wells are always dangerous because they are easily contaminated with sewage. Bacteria in the urban water supply are important because a few pathogenic species are capable of surviving, and may be distributed in cold water. The most serious of these is *Salmon-*

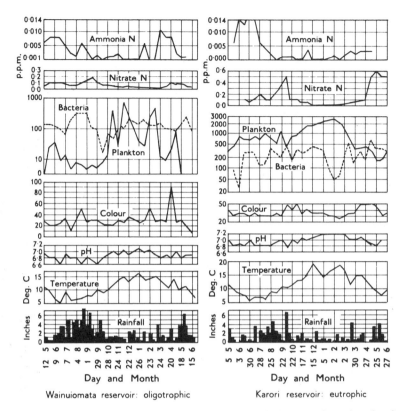

Fig. 4.6 Comparison of growth of bacteria and plankton, and nutrient levels in two New Zealand reservoirs. (After Stevenson, G., 1952, *N.Z. Jl Sci. Technol.*, **34**, 26.)

ella typhi, the bacillus of typhoid fever, which can enter a water supply only from the excreta of a person carrying the disease or actually suffering from it. Pathogens in numbers too small to be detected would be a serious hazard. However, the common and harmless intestinal bacterium, *Escherichia coli*, is present in enormous numbers in faecal matter and, though it grows only in the intestine of man and other mammals and nowhere else, it persists in water for a certain time. It can be detected readily by its growth on a special selective medium which is widely used to test water supplies for the presence of any contamination with fresh sewage or excrement. This is a specially delicate test which will show the presence of as few as one *E. coli* cell in 100 ml. of water, thus revealing any trace of sewage.

Unless the water supply is quite exceptionally pure and well protected, it is usual to treat it with sufficient chlorine to kill all the bacteria it carries before it is distributed to the users. As a rule the water is filtered first through beds of sand to remove plankton. The most useful examination of water supplies for their safety consists simply of routine counting of the numbers of bacteria which will grow per unit volume under standard conditions. Any sudden change from the normal is then readily detected and is an immediate indication of unusual and possibly dangerous conditions.

The *oceans* contain many bacteria which flourish best near the coast where drainage water and sewage increase the available nutrients. Some grow at considerable depths where the pressure is high, and many grow at low temperatures. They convert the waste organic matter in the same way as fresh-water bacteria do.

Sewage

The treatment of sewage depends on the activity of bacteria and a few fungi. Both aerobic and anaerobic saprophytes grow vigorously on the organic wastes, bringing about a similar cycle of changes to those occurring in soil or in fresh water. Bacteriophages are a feature of sewage works where they occur in quantity, and where they may be important in removing the concentration of bacterial cells from the final effluent.

Sewage is a heavily polluted mixture of water-borne wastes including both organic and inorganic material from domestic and industrial sources. By the time it reaches sewage-treatment works it is already undergoing microbial digestion and is usually more or less offensive and potentially dangerous. Nevertheless local authorities have ever-increasing amounts of it to deal with. The first treatment is a simple screening to remove coarse waste and sand. Then sewage is settled for 3–15 hours in large sedimentation tanks where the coarser solids form a sludge at the bottom.

The supernatant liquid containing dissolved organic and inorganic compounds and fine colloidal material is then commonly treated by distribution through sprinklers on to biological filters. These are large beds 4–6 ft deep filled with coke or clinker, on the surface of which purifying organisms grow in a gelatinous film. Within the filter there is a stratification of biological populations. Bacteria such as *Zoogloea ramigera* form the base of the slime mass of the upper layers in which such fungi as *Fusarium* spp. and *Geotrichum* spp. are common. Nitrifying organisms are abundant in the lower layers where the percolating liquid is much purer.

Many small animals, particularly worms and insect larvae, are important in the cycle of purification. The whole population of these filter beds is an integrated community supported by the waste materials which are converted into living substance. The effluent which contains a very low level of solutes and relatively few residual bacteria and phages can be discharged safely into rivers.

The sludge from the settlement tanks is a more difficult material, as it is highly putrefactive, though in some places it is dried for use as fertilizer. It may be dealt with by vigorous aeration to encourage rapid aerobic digestion, or it may be fermented anaerobically in enclosed tanks where methane is generated from the activities of certain obligate anaerobes. A gas mixture of useful calorific value is then recovered for heating or power supply.

The sale of modern detergents on a large scale in post-war years has raised new problems for sewage disposal. These compounds which are alkyl benzene sulphonates include some which are resistant to biological oxidation and which therefore persist through the sewage-treatment processes, causing excessive foaming which prevents sludge settlement, and also producing other difficulties and hazards. The nature of the alkyl chain on the benzene sulphonate molecule determines whether it is readily degraded by microbial action or not. Some countries, such as West Germany, have legislated to prohibit the manufacture of resistant types of alkyl benzene sulphonates, though others have relied on persuading manufacturers to avoid the undesirable substances. With the rapid increase in the development of new drugs, fungicides, insecticides and substances for other purposes, sewage treatment works are likely to face many similar problems, so that continuous testing of new compounds, not only for their uses but also for their ultimate disposal, is necessary.

5

Special Relationships between Different Organisms

As all fungi and most bacteria are heterotrophic they depend ultimately on other living organisms for food. Saprophytic organisms live only on dead material, but where fungi and bacteria take organic food substances directly from other living organisms they are called *parasites*. Where these cause some degree of injury or damage they are called *pathogens*. The organisms which supply the food and suffer in some way are called *hosts*. *Obligate parasites* are organisms completely dependent on a living host outside which they cannot grow. Many parasitic fungi and bacteria, however, are *facultative parasites* because they can grow either on a living host, or on its dead remains or on other organic substrates. Within this latter category there are organisms which are active parasites and weak saprophytes, those which are vigorous both as parasites and as saprophytes, and also some which are normally saprophytes but which may occasionally under some conditions become parasitic. Besides the varying degrees of parasitism there are a number of important examples of a balanced relationship between a micro-organism and a higher plant, or between two micro-organisms, which results when they live in close association without apparent disease and usually with apparent mutual benefit. This condition is called *symbiosis* or, by some authorities, *controlled parasitism*. Higher animals sometimes carry or house micro-organisms to which they give food and shelter without being damaged by them, a condition which is described by animal pathologists as *commensalism*.

EPIPHYTIC MICRO-ORGANISMS

The surfaces of leaves and other parts of plants carry small amounts of dust and may have traces of nutrients exuded from the living cells of the epidermis. Numerous saprophytes are able to grow on these plant surfaces as *epiphytes*. They may do little harm but if they become so abundant as to reduce the light and air reaching the leaves, they may become damaging. The commonest epiphytes on leaves are the mirror yeasts, species of *Sporobolomyces* and the related *Tilletiopsis. Cladosporium herbarum* and other *Cladosporium* species, also very abundant imperfect fungi which contribute a major part of the air-spora, occur commonly as epiphytes on grass and other leaves, but in addition luxuriate as saprophytes, and often it is not easy to determine how they are growing. Frequently they are associated with aphid attack. Leaves may become thickly covered with dark mycelium-bearing sooty spores, making partly epiphytic, partly saprophytic growths called *sooty moulds*. These may load the leaves and obstruct their functions causing senescence and death, but they are never truly parasitic.

SYMBIOSIS OR CONTROLLED PARASITISM

Three classic examples of a balanced condition resulting from two organisms living in close partnership with apparent mutual benefit are to be seen in the lichens, in root nodules (p. 71) and in mycorrhizas.

Lichens

These are dual organisms formed from the very close association of an alga, or *phycobiont*, and a fungus, or *mycobiont*. These composite organisms have definite characters which enable them to be classified like single organisms, and about 16,000 species of them are probably valid though considerably more have been described (Fig. 5.1). It was generally believed that lichens were single organisms till about 100 years ago when their dual nature was established. The fungi involved, which are most often Ascomycetes and in a few cases only are Basidiomycetes, are not found outside the lichen to which they belong, and though they may be grown in pure culture they make very slow progress. The algal partner is usually a simple green unicell and is often a species of *Trebouxia*. A few lichens in which the algal partner is a member of the Cyanophyceae are gelatinous.

Structure of lichen thallus

In some lichens (especially the gelatinous species) the fungal hyphae and *gonidia*, as the algal cells are called from an originally mistaken idea

4

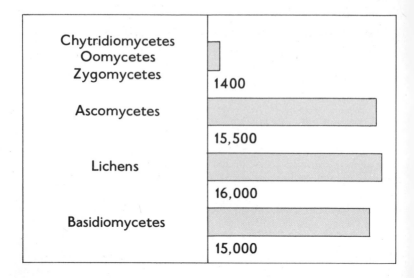

Fig. 5.1 Comparison of numbers of species in different classes. (Data from Ainsworth, G. C., 1963, *A Dictionary of the Fungi*, Commonwealth Mycological Institute, Kew.)

of their function, are equally distributed in the thallus, which is then said to be **homoiomerous**. In most lichens the algal cells are restricted to a definite layer and the lichen is said to be **heteromerous**. In these, fungal hyphae grow woven together in a plectenchyma which forms a compact outer layer or **upper cortex**. The gonidial layer lies between this cortex and a loosely woven medulla. A dense lower cortical layer may or may not be developed (Fig. 5.2). Small cups called **cyphellae** which may serve for aeration are present on the under surface of many foliose species. The three main types of these dual organisms are:

1 **Crustose lichens** which grow in a thin layer, often appearing like a splash of paint, encrusting stones or rocks.
2 **Foliose lichens** which grow epiphytically on rocks or trees, in the form of leafy, lobed structures (Fig. 5.3a).
3 **Fruticose lichens** which have freely branching thalli forming thread-like or twig-like tufts (Fig. 5.3b).

Reproduction

Within the compound thallus each partner may multiply in its characteristic manner, the algal cells growing and dividing by simple fission,

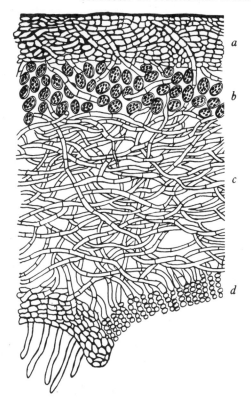

Fig. 5.2   Diagram of a section of a foliose lichen : (a) upper cortex ; (b) gonidial layer ; (c) medulla ; (d) part of a cyphella in the lower cortex.

while typical fungal fructifications bearing only fungal spores are developed on the surface. The lichen also produces structures peculiar to itself. *Soredia* which develop on the surface of many species appear as a greyish powder formed of small rounded bodies, each containing one or more algal cells enveloped by a weft of hyphae. Many lichen thalli also form tiny coral-like buds called *isidia*. Both kinds of structure are dispersed by wind or rain and serve for vegetative reproduction. Each will grow to a new lichen thallus if it is lodged in a suitable place. Larger fragments of established thalli may also be distributed to start new growths.

The physiology of lichens

Although still incompletely explored, the physiology of lichens is of special interest because these plants fill an otherwise unoccupied ecological niche where conditions for survival and growth are most difficult. The

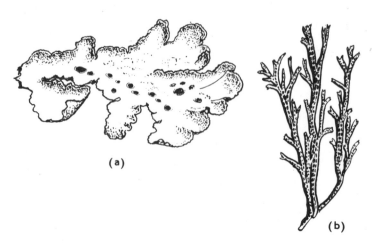

Fig. 5.3 Types of lichen thalli : (a) *Sticta* sp., a foliose lichen ($\times \frac{2}{3}$) ; (b) *Cladonia* sp., a fruticose lichen ($\times \frac{2}{3}$).

partnership has properties distinct from those of the separate organisms. Fungi are apparently the dominant partners in lichens, but while fungi are found mainly in warm, protected environments lichens flourish in cold exposed places where they may be the principal or even the only plants. The tundra vegetation of the Arctic consists largely of *Cladonia rangiferina*, known as reindeer moss, but which is a fruticose lichen on which the reindeer herds feed. *Lecanora esculenta* is the edible manna lichen of the Orient and lost explorers have survived in the New Zealand bush by eating edible lichens.

Most fungi grow best away from the light, but many of the tough lichens thrive under full exposure. Most withstand extreme drought but grow very slowly so that certain thalli have been estimated to be thousands of years old; however, some which are common under moist-temperate conditions in countries such as New Zealand grow relatively quickly. Lichens are often strongly pigmented, e.g. *Xanthoria parietina*, the paint spot lichen. Many others have been used for dyeing textiles. The universally important pH indicator litmus is extracted from *Roccella montaignei*. On the whole lichens are very sensitive to atmospheric conditions and disappear from districts where the air is polluted, except for a few such as the crustose species, *Lecanora conizaeoides*, which is common in large industrial centres, and *Stereocaulon pileatum* which may also grow in such places. Lichens absorb water vapour from the atmosphere and take up ions in solution with great rapidity which is probably the basis for their sensitivity to atmospheric pollution. Many characteristically produce complex organic acids known as lichen acids. A substance known as usnic acid which has been prepared from some *Cladonia* species is a recently discovered broad-spectrum antibiotic. Similar substances may help to preserve the long-lived lichens.

Though the fungi and algae of most lichens can be cultured separately they do not readily form a compound thallus when cultures are mixed. Special minimal conditions for growth are apparently necessary before the combination develops. As the fungus appears to be the dominant partner the modern trend is to classify lichens within the fungi where most of them are fitted into the Ascomycetes, a much smaller number falling into place among the Basidiomycetes.

Mycorrhizas

Mycorrhizas (literally, fungus-roots) are complex structures of healthy plant roots and fungal hyphae. Two types of this symbiotic association are recognized.

Ectotrophic mycorrhizas

Almost all forest trees, both Gymnosperms and Angiosperms, under natural conditions have ectotrophic mycorrhizas. These develop from short branch roots which fork repeatedly and often grow as coralloid structures (Fig. 5.4) in which the cortex contains many intercellular hyphae connec-

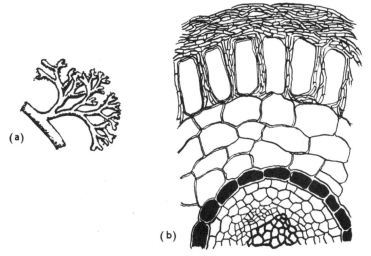

(a)

(b)

Fig. 5.4 (a) Sketch of coralloid ectotrophic mycorrhiza of *Pinus* (× 6) (b) Diagram of a section of *Nothofagus* ectotrophic mycorrhiza with fungal mantle and intercellular hyphae (× 125).

ted with a well-developed external mycelium. This forms a mantle on the outer surface of the short root and replaces the piliferous layer with its root hairs. The fungi concerned are mostly members of the Agaricales, usually one or a few species being associated with one species of tree. The characteristic toadstools of the fungi may appear under the tree in autumn. Foresters have long recognized the importance of mycorrhizas in the nutrition of forest trees which do not thrive without suitable fungi, though they may be cultivated successfully without fungi in specially enriched soil. It has been shown that mycorrhizas absorb nutrient ions more efficiently than non-mycorrhizal roots. The mycorrhizal fungi in culture have been found to require B-group vitamins which they may get from the tree roots along with carbohydrates, so that both partners probably benefit from the association.

Endotrophic mycorrhizas

These are found on a wide range of herbaceous plants as well as on a few woody species. The infected roots contain well-developed hyphae running in the intercellular spaces and penetrating many of the living cortical cells. External hyphae may be only scantily developed. All orchids have endotrophic mycorrhizas and in the roots of most the endophytic fungus is a species of *Rhizoctonia*, a genus which includes a number of pathogens. In a few orchid species the fungus is *Armillaria mellea*, the boot-lace fungus which is also a notorious tree pathogen. The infection begins in the germinating orchid seed which is exceptionally small, and which normally does not grow till it has been invaded by a suitable strain of fungus, after which progress is very slow. It may be months or years before a normal green seedling appears. In the cortex of older roots a layer of apparently healthy living cells may be seen, all containing coils of hyphae, named **pelotons**, which gradually become clumped and then disintegrate. Often they are filled with oily material which appears to pass to the root cells when the hyphae disappear. Some brown orchids lacking chlorophyll, such as the European *Neottia nidus-avis*, the bird's nest orchid, and species of *Gastrodia* found in eastern Asia and Australasia, live completely saprophytically on soil-organic matter and other nutrients absorbed and digested by means of their mycorrhizas which in some cases contain *A. mellea*. In some orchids the fungus in the roots has been found to show seasonal fluctuation. Some cultivated orchids are raised successfully in aseptic culture without mycorrhizas by supplying the seeds with a suitable nutrient solution including sugar, which in these cases is a satisfactory substitute for the living fungus.

Many members of the Ericaceae and closely related families, including all the heaths and rhododendrons, have endotrophic mycorrhizas similar to those of orchids. Hyphae are well developed in a region of the root cortex where pelotons are formed in many cells (Fig. 5.5). The endophyte may not be restricted to the roots, but may also extend into the intercellular spaces of all the aerial parts of the plant, even infecting the seed in the ovary, but without causing injury. These plants cannot be grown normally without their mycorrhizal fungus and are restricted to acid soils in which they can develop.

Fig. 5.5 Diagram of section of *Dracophyllum* (Epacridaceae) endotrophic mycorrhiza with pelotons (×150).

Arbuscular-vesicular mycorrhizas

The roots of numerous herbaceous plants including grasses and many crop plants contain endophytic 'Phycomycete' fungi. Species of *Endogone* and *Pythium* have been found associated with different roots. These fungi form thick, and often irregular, nonseptate hyphae running in the intercellular spaces of the root cortex. Temporary developments of hyphal processes either in the form of finely branching masses known as **arbuscules** or as simple, swollen vesicles are seen inside older cortical cells, so this type of mycorrhiza is called **arbuscular-vesicular** (Fig. 5.6). It is likely that food material passes from these structures, as they disappear, into the cortical cells which are well nourished and have conspicuous nuclei. Experiments have shown that under poor nutrient conditions plants with endotrophic mycorrhiza make better growth than control plants without infection. There is also evidence indicating that under certain conditions some mycorrhizas may fix nitrogen.

It is an interesting fact that species of both *Rhizoctonia* and *Pythium* are well-known root parasites which may cause damping-off disease of young seedlings, and *Armillaria mellea* (p. 51) is also a root parasite. The balance between the condition of disease on the one hand, and a mutually beneficial partnership on the other, in some cases appears to be controlled by the external conditions, though different strains of fungi may be involved in different relationships. The condition of mycorrhiza, which is widespread along land plants, appears also to be a very ancient one in their geological history. Some very early Pteridophyte fossils show coils of fungi preserved in cortical cells of undamaged roots or rhizomes. As many living Pteridophytes have mycorrhizas or mycorrhizal rhizomes of similar appearance, it seems likely that the fossil plants were mycorrhizal also, although the relationship could be an ancient example of plant disease.

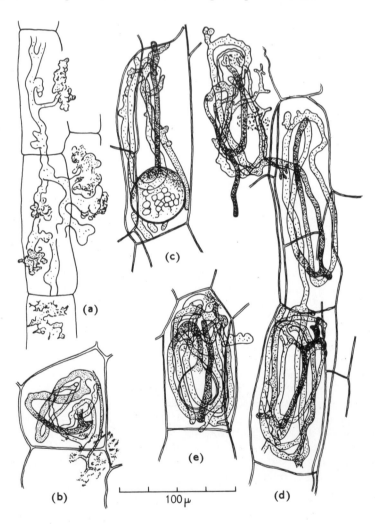

Fig. 5.6 Arbuscular-vesicular endotrophic mycorrhiza : (a and b) of *Viola* ; (c–e) of *Taxus*. (After original drawings by Rosemary Thomas.)

PHYTOPATHOLOGY

Many fungal parasites may cause diseases on the higher plants on which they grow. A few bacteria also attack and damage various higher plants while a number of viruses produce serious plant diseases. Severe physiological diseases of plants are less common than those due to parasites, and are brought about by unfavourable conditions for growth such as unbalanced nutrition, usually an insufficient supply of some essential element, the presence of poisons or unbalanced water relations. In agriculture, horticulture and forestry, plant diseases may cause serious losses and frequently special treatments for control and protection are necessary.

Obligate and facultative parasites

The *degree of dependence* of the parasitic organism on the host varies greatly, and so does the amount of damage it causes. The rust and powdery mildew fungi and a few others are obligate parasites which can grow only on a living host. Usually they have very specialized nutritional requirements so that they can grow only on one species, or even a single variety of higher plant. Some obligate parasites grow as a systemic infection extend-

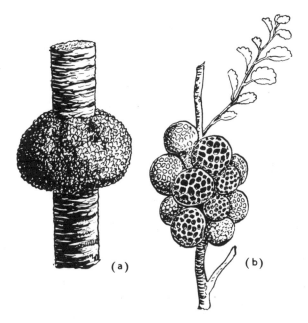

Fig. 5.7 *Cyttaria gunnii* on *Nothofagus menziesii* : (a) perennial woody gall($\times \frac{1}{6}$);
(b) annual spring crop of ascocarps on a small gall ($\times \frac{5}{8}$).

ing throughout the host but in others the growth may be restricted to a small part of the host which, although it is damaged to some extent locally, continues to live and support the parasite. The hyphae of these fungi may invade the host through stomata or by direct penetration of the cuticle. Occasionally they enter through wounds. Inside the host the parasitic hyphae grow between the cells producing haustoria which intrude into the living host cells without breaking their plasmalemmas. They obtain food from these cells without killing them. The total volume of fungal growth may not be very large and it may be confined to a small part of the host causing a local lesion of limited extent. Nevertheless the obligate parasites such as the rusts and mildews sporulate freely on the plant surfaces and spread widely often causing serious economic loss by weakening plants and reducing yield.

If the host cells are killed by a rust fungus or other obligate parasite then the disease fails to develop because the host is **hypersensitive.** In this case the host is resistant to the disease which never becomes established. Obligate parasites, especially some of the rusts, may interfere with the growth-regulating mechanism causing the host cells to multiply making hypertrophied organs or definite galls which accommodate more fungal colonies (Figs. 5.7, 5.8). Even with such extensive development of the parasite, death of the host does not usually result from the infection.

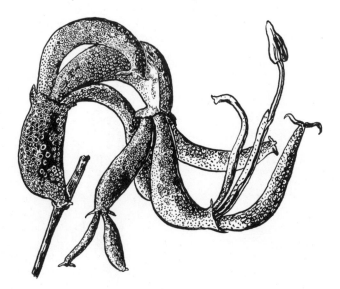

Fig. 5.8 Grossly distorted inflorescence of *Clematis paniculata* infected by the rust fungus *Aecidium otagense* ($\times \frac{2}{3}$).

The **smut** fungi, e.g. those species of *Ustilago* which cause loose smut of grain, are facultative parasites which can be cultured with considerable difficulty, but do not usually produce normal growths in the laboratory and are not known to grow saprophytically in nature. They resemble obligate parasites in having a limited host range and in forming infections which may have a limited effect at first. They may, however, be sufficiently numerous in grain crops to be serious. In some species, e.g. *U. nuda*, causing loose smut of barley, spores carried to flowers grow to form a small amount of resting mycelium which remains in the ripened grain. When the seed germinates the fungus grows sparsely within the seedling causing no visible damage till the new grain is ripening. Then the fungus develops rapidly and produces a large mass of sooty spores which take the place of the grain (see also p. 155).

Fig 5.9 Potato leaf blighted by *Phytophthora infestans* ($\times \frac{1}{3}$).

Some facultative parasites which may be cultured readily grow weakly under natural conditions outside their main host. *Ophiobolus graminis*, which infects roots of wheat and so causes take-all disease, does not survive long in soil unless suitable roots are present. If arable land carries weed grasses this very damaging disease may persist in a rotation from one wheat crop to the next. It can survive on grass roots growing weakly without causing much damage to the grass, but when wheat roots are present it may grow in them exceedingly well, with the disastrous results indicated by the popular name. As a saprophyte in the soil *O. graminis* grows feebly and is soon eliminated in competition with vigorous saprophytes.

The potato blight fungus *Phytophthora infestans* (p. 128) is a notorious example of a facultative parasite of strictly limited host range, capable of growing vigorously on living potato plants (Fig. 5.9) or of overwintering in tubers or plant remains. It is readily cultured. Most infected tubers die (many from secondary infections) but some may survive with a small amount of internal mycelium which grows within the new plant produced by the sprouting tuber in spring. Soon the mycelium spreads in the new foliage and, if warm, humid conditions prevail, sporangiophores grow out through the stomata forming single-celled sporangia, which are shed and may infect other plants. If this disease starts early in a wet summer most plants of the crop may be completely killed by the fungus. The ravages of potato blight when first introduced into Europe had tragic results for the peasants, especially the Irish, who had come to depend on their potato crop. A full and lively account of the story is given by Large in *The Advance of the Fungi*.

Other facultative parasites such as species of *Pythium* or *Botrytis cinerea* among the fungi, or *Pectobacterium* species, grow equally well on a range of different plants, or on plant remains, and may be cultured on various media. Such parasites may be very destructive and rapidly kill their hosts. They invade the plant tissues on a broad front. The mycelium of the fungi, or the bacterial colonies, produce pectin-hydrolysing enzymes which spread ahead of the advancing parasite, dissolving the middle lamellae of the cell walls, so causing a soft rot of the plant tissues. The disorganized cells soon die and the whole organ, or even complete plant, collapses. Soft rotting organisms are often secondary parasites. If potato tubers are invaded by *Phytophthora infestans* they are open to attack by *Pectobacterium* species which may quickly reduce the whole tuber to a useless mush, although the bacterium is not able to gain entry to an uninjured tuber.

Bacterial diseases

Bacteria causing disease in plants are usually able to attack a series of different hosts. *Bacterium tumefaciens* causes crown gall on a wide range of cultivated plants, especially fruit trees. Fire blight which commonly attacks pears, but occurs also on various other fruit and ornamental trees, is caused by *B. amylovorum* which may be carried by pollinating insects. It enters through the style or through nectaries and grows throughout complete branches or entire plants with great rapidity, killing them. This disease has been known for many years in America and New Zealand but has appeared in Britain only recently. Angular leaf spot of tobacco (Plate 5B) is a more specialized bacterial disease due to infection of leaves through the stomata by *Pseudomonas angulata*. Each bacterial colony kills a small angular piece of leaf.

Virus diseases

Viruses causing plant diseases may spread all through the plant, mainly via the xylem and phloem, leading to a systemic infection, the result of which may be stunting, distorting and/or discolouring, but plants are seldom killed immediately. The same virus may infect different plants causing different symptoms in each. One virus may have many different strains, each of which produces symptoms of differing severity in the same host. Often aphids or other leaf-sucking insects transmit viruses from one plant to another, though they can be spread by mechanical rubbing or by activities such as pruning, and they are also known to be carried in soil. More than one virus may be present in a single plant, but often systemic infection with one virus prevents development of the symptoms of a second should it gain entry. This may be a beneficial effect when the first virus causes slight or negligible disease. Seed of lettuce may carry virus infection, but in most other plants the systemic virus does not reach the ovary and so is not inherited by one generation from its predecessors, but plants propagated vegetatively such as the potato are always in danger of carrying viruses. On this account potato culture in England depends on certified 'seed' potatoes imported from Scotland, where virus infections are rigorously rogued. Since few aphids survive the cool climate the rogued crops remain free from disease.

Diseases in agriculture, horticulture and forestry

In *agriculture* many plant diseases have to be reckoned with. Rusts and mildews which attack the foliage of grain crops may seriously reduce the

Fig. 5.10 Wart disease of potato caused by *Synchytrium endobioticum* ($\times \frac{1}{3}$).

yield. The grain itself may be infected by smut, *Ustilago* spp. or *Tilletia* spp. which make it useless, or by ergot, *Claviceps purpurea*, which turns each infected grain into a dangerously poisonous fungal stroma. If the roots are destroyed by *Ophiobolus graminis*, take-all, many plants may be killed. Eye-spot of wheat due to *Cercosporella herpotrichoides* attacks the crown of the plant which may be killed or weakened so that areas of the crop are lodged, and therefore are difficult to harvest and liable to rot in wet seasons. The potato plant, which is important in the agriculture of all temperate countries, is subject to a number of diseases. Potato blight is the one which may reach disastrous proportions in a bad season destroying whole fields. Scab due to *Streptomyces scabies* and wart disease caused by *Synchytrium endobioticum* disfigures tubers (Fig. 5.10), the latter seriously. Virus diseases are of special importance in potatoes because they occur regularly with large reduction in yield.

In **horticulture** many diseases are encountered attacking fruit, flowers or vegetables. In these crops it is often the part of the plant most easily and frequently damaged which is reaped for sale, so that a degree of infection which would be of little account in agriculture is here a serious concern. Leaves are attacked by a variety of leaf-spot or leaf-scab organisms, as well as by rusts and mildews. Stems and roots are also subject to damage (Plate 8A). Wilt diseases which block the vascular tissue are important in various plants, particularly tomatoes and carnations. Clubroot of crucifers caused by *Plasmodiophora brassicae* may cause severe stunting. Many viruses have damaging results including several, such as streak of tulips, which disfigure flowers, yet variegation of foliage due to virus infection may be prized (p. 23). Damping-off of seedlings due to destruction of the hypocotyl by one of the common facultative parasites, particularly *Pythium*, *Rhizoctonia* or *Botrytis*, is often important especially where early crops are required.

In **forestry** damping-off of seedlings is occasionally troublesome in forest nurseries. Foliage diseases are fairly common and may be disfiguring without seriously affecting the crop. On broad-leaved trees the fungi concerned with leaf spots are usually Ascomycetes, such as *Rhytisma acerinum* which causes tar spot of sycamore and maples (Fig. 5.11). Mildews are also widely developed on broad-leaved trees, particularly late in the growing season, but they are not known on conifers. Rusts occur on both dicotyledonous trees and Gymnosperms, and most have a complex life cycle occurring also on alternate hosts. One of special importance is *Cronartium ribicola*, currant and gooseberry rust, which forms its uredio- and teliospores on these hosts, and its aeciospores on five-needled pines (p. 158). In America *Ribes* bushes commonly grow as under-shrubs in pine forests from which they must be eliminated to prevent spores spreading to the pines, because this rust may cause serious damage and even kill the trees. Galls and burls are occasionally produced on wood by various parasites. These are deforming and weakening to some extent, but may yield useful timber of fancy grain. Stem decay due to Basidiomycetes, especially members of the Aphyllophorales, the bracket fungi, regularly causes death of standing trees. Roots may be attacked by *Armillaria mellea* (Fig. 3.2a) which may kill all kinds of woody plants. Soft woods are occasionally destroyed by root rot due to species of *Phytophthora*.

Fig. 5.11 Tar spot of *Acer pseudoplatanus* (sycamore) caused by *Rhytisma acerinum* ($\times \frac{1}{3}$).

Control of plant diseases

The control of disease is an important consideration in the cultivation of plants. Where large numbers of identical plants are brought together and maintained under the best possible conditions for luxuriant growth and high yield, an opportunity exists for the spread of parasites which are of little account under natural conditions. A vigorous plant is not necessarily more resistant to disease than a poorly-developed one, and may in fact offer more opportunity to parasites of above-ground parts, though vigorous plants may better withstand root parasites. Defence measures must be economic to be practicable. Often control methods which are too expensive for large-scale agriculture can be used profitably in intensive horticulture where the value of the crops is higher. Where a disease is well known the risks involved can be weighed and defence may begin at the precautionary stage. The practice of clean cultivation to remove trash, ground keepers, self-sown crop plants and weeds which may carry disease, the use of clean or certified seed, and of resistant varieties are all important measures. Preventive treatments such as seed disinfection are often cheap and effective and have been very successful in killing spores on grain and other types of seed. Chemical sprays and dusts are applied on a wide scale to the surface of plants to prevent penetration by plant pathogens.

For soil-borne diseases rotation of crops is of great importance provided that susceptible species of weeds are eliminated as far as possible. This is the main measure against take-all disease of wheat. Where infection persists for long periods in soil, even in the absence of any host, simple rotation is not effective. *Synchytrium endobioticum* for example can survive in soil for many years, but varieties of potato resistant to wart disease may be grown safely on land known to be contaminated. *Plasmodiophora brassicae* which causes clubroot of *Brassicas* persists for long periods in soil, but may be suppressed by liming, and roots of young plants may be treated with chemical compounds before setting out. In horticulture a common practice is partial sterilization of soil, which is important in killing many parasites, especially damping-off and wilt fungi, and has the additional favourable effects of killing weed seeds and increasing fertility. Many beneficial bacteria are left in the soil the texture of which is also improved. In glasshouse management the top layer of soil is treated on a large scale by steam which heats the ground sufficiently to kill the residual parasites. Various chemical disinfectants may also be used but the majority are more expensive.

If air-borne infection, such as rust of wheat, is carried from a great distance it is more difficult for the farmer to protect his crops. The distribution depends on high-altitude air currents, for information about which meteorological observations are necessary. Climate and weather are very important in the development and spread of plant diseases, especially of the leaf-infecting fungi. Warm humid conditions favour development of sporangiospores of *Phytophthora infestans* causing potato blight, *Plasmopara viticola* causing vine mildew, or of other downy mildews. Chemical sprays are often used to prevent the spread of mildews, especially on vines. In this connection scientific advice is usually given to farmers by radio when outbreaks of plant diseases are likely.

Severe infection in a potato crop is difficult to halt as protective spraying is usually damaging, though it is sometimes resorted to. If plants are already well developed, often the most economical practice is to save the tubers by killing the above-ground part of the plants, together with the fungus they carry, by spraying with sulphuric acid, a comparatively inexpensive treatment. At the end of every wet summer potato fields may be seen with rows of blackened haulms which have been so treated. A great range of chemical substances is now available for use in controlling pathogens. Pre-war treatments were mainly based on compounds of either copper or sulphur, but these are being partly replaced by many different organic compounds which are prepared for use as sprays to coat the plant surface with a thin film, or as finely divided powders for dusting. Bacterial diseases which develop altogether inside the plant tissues cannot be reached by surface treatment. A modern development important in this connection is the use of systemic fungicides or bactericides which will spread throughout the plant tissues without damaging them. The antibiotics griseofulvin and streptomycin are the most promising compounds so far available for giving plants a systemic protection. Streptomycin has proved useful against fire blight in New Zealand.

The virus diseases raise special problems in control. No practical method is yet known for treating a virus once it enters a plant, but use may be made of the important fact that one more or less harmless virus infection may prevent the development of a second serious disease virus. The original reason for the resistance of the King Edward strain of potato to certain damaging virus diseases was discovered to be that it was already infected with a virus which had apparently no ill effects. More recently King Edward potato plants have been grown from tissue cultures free from virus and experimental crops have been greatly increased. The main defence measures so far used against virus disease in plants are designed to control the insects which transmit them, though the best protection is the use of resistant varieties. It is also important to prevent the spread of virus diseases by the elimination of rogues and weeds which may provide a reservoir of infection. Modern chemical herbicides and insecticides are invaluable for controlling these sources of infection. True seed is almost always free from virus even if taken from heavily infected crops, but where propagation by vegetative methods is practised clean stocks should be used.

Official control of growing, and of import and export of plants, is very important in restricting disease which may already exist in some areas, so preventing it from spreading into surrounding states or countries. Government regulations are in effect in practically all countries and the inspectors who enforce the regulations may have wide powers. Where necessary, destruction of infected crops may be ordered, and often on a smaller scale the most satisfactory and inexpensive treatment for a diseased plant is simply to dig it up and burn it.

HUMAN AND ANIMAL MYCOSES

Most parasitic diseases of higher animals are due to bacteria or viruses. Their study is included in medical science and is outside the scope of this work, but a few animal diseases of importance are caused by fungi. The highly contagious skin infection, ringworm, which may infect many domestic mammals, hedgehogs and man, may be due to species of three different genera, *Microsporum*, *Trichophyton* and *Epidermophyton* which are able to digest and utilize keratin, the protein of the horny outer layers of the skin, hair and nails. These dermatophytes do not invade the underlying tissues but make a limited mycelial growth in the epidermis. Other

Trichophyton spp. may infect the skin between the toes causing athlete's foot (e.g. *T. interdigitale*), or the skin of the scalp or the hair itself.

Various normally saprophytic species of *Aspergillus, Penicillium, Mucor* and *Rhizopus* may grow within the tissues of various animals, particularly in the lungs, causing diseases to which the general name **mycoses** (sing. mycosis) is given, or when *Aspergillus* spp. are involved the name **aspergillosis** is used. *A. fumigatus* is the most important species. Farmer's lung (p. 74), a serious disease resembling tuberculosis, is occasionally a mycosis or aspergillosis which may develop in people who have worked with mouldy hay. Birds are especially susceptible to pulmonary aspergillosis which is often fatal to penguins in captivity or to brooder chicks. Cattle may become infected in the lungs or in abdominal organs by species of *Mucor* or *Rhizopus* which cause serious disease. Some species of the fungus *Candida* growing in a yeast-like form become parasitic on man or other animals. They often cause secondary infections on patients weakened by some other disease or condition and then may attack the skin on damp folds on the body, or the mucous membranes.

FUNGAL TOXINS

Certain fungi produce compounds which are poisonous to animals and may have serious effects on them. Several species of Agaricales produce poisonous fructifications which may cause distress, or even death, if eaten. The common condition of 'hay fever', usually caused by pollen, may also be caused by certain fungal spores to which some people are more sensitive than they are to the common pollens. *Claviceps purpurea* which causes ergot in grain (Fig. 3.5) contains a powerful poison. When infected grain has been used for flour or meal, people eating it have suffered an acute condition known as St. Anthony's Fire, and some have even died. Infection of stored peanuts with *Aspergillus flavus* resulted in poisoning many domestic birds and mammals when the nuts were used in England in 1960 for fodder. Many turkey poults died. A group of compounds named aflatoxins which have been recovered from ground nuts inoculated with *A. flavus* have been shown to cause severe liver damage. Thus any mouldy food is potentially dangerous.

Facial eczema

This is a puzzling disease of sheep and cattle that has been known for 50 years in the North Island of New Zealand where it has resulted in widespread economic loss. Under warm, humid conditions in some districts during certain seasons, the rapidly growing pastures produce a toxin which causes severe liver damage in grazing animals. The result of this damage is failure to eliminate phylloerythrin, a chlorophyll derivative, which accumulates in the skin causing photosensitization. The visual symptoms of facial eczema then follow in affected animals. Recent research has shown that the toxin is produced by abundantly sporing strains of a common saprophytic fungus, *Pithomyces chartarum*, the black spores of which (Fig. 5.12) contain

Fig. 5.12   Black poisonous conidia of *Pithomyces chartarum* (Fungi Imperfecti) (×1,000).

a compound called sporodesmin. A dose of 100 µg of the pure toxin has produced severe liver damage in a guinea-pig. An indication of how severely damaged the liver of a sheep may become after it has grazed pasture containing the fungus is shown in Plate 7.

ENTOMOGENOUS FUNGI

Some entire families and other groups of fungal species are parasites of insects. The Entomophthorales of the Zygomycetes may be illustrated by *Entomophthora muscae*, which formerly commonly attacked house-flies in autumn when it was to be seen growing as a whitish halo round a moribund insect. Modern use of DDT has practically eliminated this by killing flies before infection develops so that a negligible source of infection remains. The numerous species of the Laboulbeniales of the Ascomycetes are highly specialized superficial parasites on insects. Species of the genus *Cordyceps*, which is related to the genus *Claviceps* causing ergot, parasitize different insects, spiders, and often larvae developing underground. The contents of the arthropod body are transformed into a sclerotium inside the animal's skin, so that finally a myco-mummy is produced. From this body elongated stromata may grow up bearing perithecia and ascospores. In some places these vegetable caterpillars may be found underground where single or branching spore-bearing horns appear out of the soil (Figs. 5.13, 5.14).

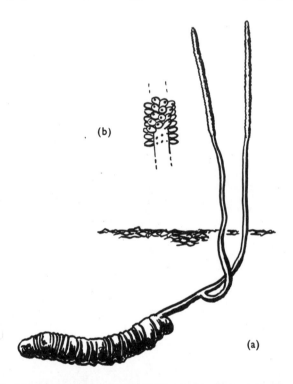

Fig. 5.13 *Cordyceps robertsii*: (a) habit of vegetable caterpillar sclerotium with stroma bearing perithecia ($\times \frac{2}{3}$); (b) detail of clustered perithecia ($\times 4$).

Species of *Aschersonia* of the Fungi Imperfecti, which are parasitic on insects, have been used in Florida, where there is a warm, humid climate, for the biological control of scale insects but without spectacular success. The genus *Septobasidium* belongs to a small Basidiomycete family the species of which are parasitic on colonies of scale insects, which they do not kill, but render sterile. A curious relationship develops. The fungus forms a perennial hyphal mat under which a colony of scale insects survives. Species of *Isaria*, a genus of the Fungi Imperfecti, attack insects and are found commonly in some places on various pupae or on dead cicada nymphs which remain buried while fungal **coremia** grow above ground (Fig. 5.14b). A coremium is a bundle of hyphae, more or less joined together, producing spores.

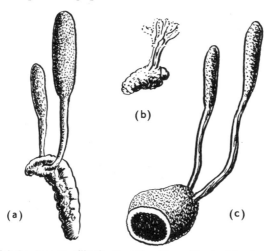

Fig. 5.14 (a) *Cordyceps militaris* stromata with perithecia rising from mummified insect ($\times 1\frac{1}{3}$). (b) *Isaria* on insect nymph ($\times 1$). (c) *C. ophioglossoides* on *Elaphomyces granulatus* (part cut away) ($\times \frac{2}{3}$).

Fungi associated with insects

The nests of ants and termites are built from such materials as soil, litter and partly digested wood which naturally carry a rich mycoflora. However, special kinds of fungi found nowhere else also grow in these nests. Sometimes the insects feed on the fungus or even, in the case of the South American leaf-cutting ants, they cultivate it. These ants gather leaves which are cut, chewed and then 'planted' in 'fungus gardens' where special edible toadstools grow. Adults and larvae feed on the young fructifications. The termites or white ants of tropical Africa and Asia build large nests of woody comb which becomes lined with mycelium. Old nests sprout rich crops of tall elegant agarics recognized as distinct and classified in a special genus *Termitomyces*. These are prized for human food but it is not clear that they are any use to the termites.

Some beetles which have wood-boring larvae introduce a fungus into the hole in which they lay their eggs. Female *Sirex* beetles which attack pine trees may carry mycelium of *Stereum sanguinolentum* in sacs between segments of the abdomen. When the ovipositor has bored into the wood

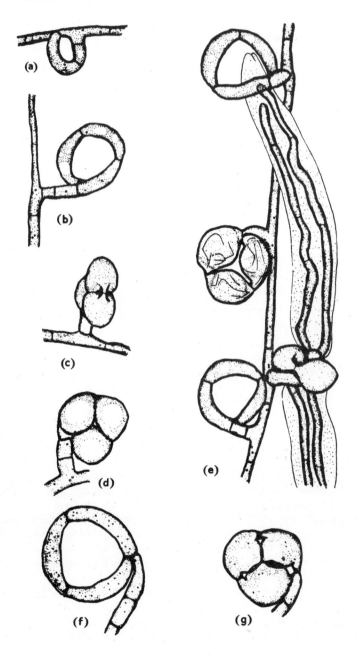

(a)

(b)

(c)

(d)

(e)

(f)

(g)

the egg is laid together with a fungus inoculum. Growth of mycelium begins first and softens the wood for the developing larva. The damage due to the fungus may be more serious than that due to the insect but the fungus gains entry only through the insect's activities. Other tree or timber diseases may be similarly spread by beetles. The Dutch elm disease caused by the fungus *Ceratostomella ulmi* which has killed many elm trees in America and Europe is spread by engraver beetles which tunnel under the bark. In this case the fungus spreads far beyond the territory occupied by the insects which carried it. The sap wood is gradually completely destroyed and old trees have been killed in 2 or 3 years.

PREDACIOUS FUNGI

A number of soil fungi have been seen actually trapping nematode worms or soil Protozoa which are held in hyphal coils or nooses. In some species of *Arthrobotrys* the hyphae growing through the soil have highly specialized branches of 3 cells which lie in a ring and form a trap for nematode worms. When a worm enters a ring the 3 cells inflate in about one-tenth of a second and hold it fast (Fig. 5.15). Later a few branch hyphae grow through the victim and digest its contents. Some other soil fungi catch tiny animals in coils of sticky hyphae. These predacious fungi are known to reproduce only by conidia and so are placed in the Fungi Imperfecti.

Fig. 5.15 Predacious fungi: (a–e) *Arthrobotrys dactyloides*: (a) developing ring; (b) unconstricted ring; (c and d) front and side views of constricted rings; (e) habit showing caught nematode penetrated by absorptive hyphae. (f and g) *Dactylella doedycoides*: (f) unconstricted ring; (g) constricted ring. (After Muller, H. G., 1958, *Trans. Br. mycol. Soc.*, **41**, 348.)

6

Microbiological Industrial Processes

Antibiotics, the wonder drugs now produced on a very large scale from cultures of various micro-organisms, have captured popular imagination although, in fact, the field of applied microbiology is still dominated by its oldest industry, that of brewing. The growth of yeast for baking bread is also on a world-wide scale. Other compounds of commercial and pharmaceutical importance are prepared in modern industrial developments from various fungi and bacteria, some of which are the source of important food supplements such as the vitamins.

FERMENTATION INDUSTRIES

The production of beer

Brewing is carried out with different media and organisms to produce the various kinds of fermented drinks which are then in a condition to be preserved. **Beer** is brewed from **malt** which is made from barley grain sprouted sufficiently for the germ to produce the necessary enzymes to hydrolyse the endospermic starch to maltose. Gibberellins are used to stimulate seedling growth and so hasten the malting process. When the sprouted grain is carefully dried, so that the tiny seedling is killed but the enzymes are not destroyed, it forms malt. In the breweries a mash prepared from ground malt and warm water is held till all the starch is digested.

The liquor, called **wort**, is drained away from the residual grain into large kettles where hops, to give flavour and antimicrobial properties, are added. After about 2 hours' boiling to extract the hops and to precipitate any protein in solution, the sterile wort is separated from the spent hops,

cooled to about 62°F, and then run into large open fermentation vats
(Fig. 6.1). Here it is seeded ('pitched' is the brewer's term) with wet
cultures of *Saccharomyces cerevisiae* or *S. carlsbergensis*, each of which has
its own special fermentation characters. Most strains of *S. cerevisiae* used
by British brewers are top yeasts which float in a mass on the tops of the
vats of beer while *S. carlsbergensis* which is widely used on the continent
of Europe is a bottom yeast, settling in a sludge at the bottom of the vats.
For the first 12–18 hours after seeding there is little growth or fermentation,

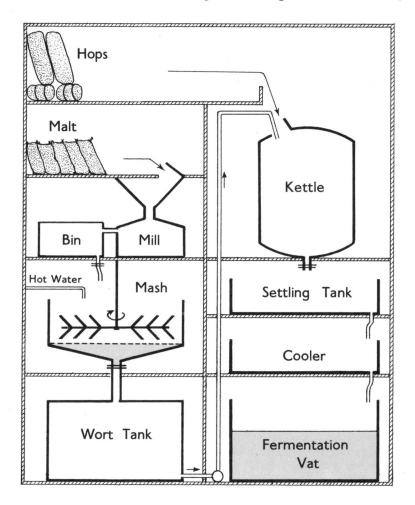

Fig. 6.1 Diagram illustrating the sequence of processes in a brewery.

then rapid development follows which generates heat so that the mixture must be cooled. Temperature control is important because it is only when the fermentation is carried out at a low temperature that all the sugar is converted to alcohol. With rapid fermentation at higher temperatures additional products undesirable in the beer are also formed. When the brew is complete, in 2–8 days, all the sugar has been converted to carbon dioxide and alcohol which reaches a concentration of 4–8 per cent. Good brewing yeast should finally flocculate from the beer leaving it clear and bright. Some yeast is kept from selected brews and used for pitching further batches. Much research has been done in an endeavour to work out a method of continuous brewing to replace the batches of each distinct stage. Some breweries have continuous-flow plants, but the method is not yet sufficiently satisfactory to be widely adopted.

Manufacture of wine

Wine making, which is almost as large an industry as the brewing of beer, depends on the fermentation of grape juice, called **must**, by wild yeasts naturally present on the skin of the fruit. Treatment of the fresh must with sulphur dioxide is designed to kill all wild micro-organisms other than the desirable *Saccharomyces cerevisiae* var. *ellipsoideus* which is a bottom yeast. The growth of grey mould, *Botrytis cinerea*, on the grape skins in late summer is a favourable infection which damages the skins allowing the grapes to dry out a little and so to give a more concentrated must. Sugar content, acidity and resin in the grape juice are factors affected by weather and which are of great importance to the fermentation. Modern scientific control enables these to be adjusted after bad summers when the must does not have a good natural composition. When the fermentation, which must be carried out slowly at a low temperature, is complete the liquor may contain 8–15 per cent alcohol, the yeast dies and the wine is stable. The ripening and maturing of the sterile wine is a slow chemical process which goes on for many years in wine cellars. A mixed growth of mould on the cellar vaults shows that temperature and humidity are favourable.

Cider from fermented apple juice, **perry** from fermented pears and other beverages are locally important. *Saké* is made in Japan from steamed rice which is first digested with the fungus *Aspergillus oryzae* in order to convert the starch to sugar. Subsequent fermentation with a special strain of *S. cerevisiae* produces a liquor with an exceptionally high alcohol content of up to 22 per cent.

Industrial alcohol has been distilled from brews of waste substances containing carbohydrate, such as molasses and wood sulphite liquor, fermented with *S. cerevisiae*, but it is being displaced by synthetic ethanol produced by the catalytic hydration of ethylene.

Bakers' strains of *S. cerevisiae* are selected for high production of carbon dioxide and are grown generally under aerobic conditions. A large industry prepares cakes of pressed yeast for bakeries.

Glycerol and other products of fermentation

Glycerol has been produced from yeast fermentation of a glucose medium to which sulphite has been added. Under these conditions a useful proportion of the dihydroxyacetone phosphate formed in glycolysis (p. 29) is reduced to glycerol.

$$
\begin{array}{l}
CH_2OH \\
| \\
C{=}O \\
| \\
CH_2OPO_3H_2 \\
\text{dihydroxy-} \\
\text{acetone phosphate}
\end{array}
\quad + NADH_2 \rightarrow \quad
\begin{array}{l}
CH_2OH \\
| \\
CHOH \\
| \\
CH_2OPO_3H_2 \\
\text{glycerol-3-phosphate}
\end{array}
\quad + NAD
$$

$$
\begin{array}{l}
CH_2OH \\
| \\
CHOH \\
| \\
CH_2OPO_3H_2 \\
\text{glycerol-3-phosphate}
\end{array}
\quad + \text{phosphatase} \rightarrow \quad
\begin{array}{l}
CH_2OH \\
| \\
CHOH \\
| \\
CH_2OH \\
\text{glycerol}
\end{array}
\quad + \text{phosphate}
$$

This process was used on a considerable scale in Germany during World War I but is no longer of economic importance.

Butanol ($CH_3CH_2CH_2CH_2OH$) has also been produced by fermentation, but the market is now more cheaply supplied with a synthetic product. Molasses with supplements of other waste materials was fermented in closed vessels anaerobically by *Clostridium acetobutylicum*. The growth of unwanted contaminant organisms was a hazard of this process and occasionally in practice infection with phages proved disastrous.

Acetic acid and *vinegar* are formed by the aerobic growth in an alcohol medium of species of two genera of bacteria, *Acetobacter* and *Acetomonas*. The industrial method of making malt vinegar, known as the 'quick vinegar' process, consists of trickling beer through towers packed with beech shavings coated by a growth of the acetifying bacteria which oxidize the alcohol.

$$CH_3CH_2OH + O_2 \rightarrow CH_3COOH + H_2O$$
ethyl alcohol   acetic acid

Lactic acid, which is used on a considerable scale in the food industry and has some other applications, is still produced solely by fermentation. A sugary medium fortified with ammonium salts is fermented in closed vessels with species of *Lactobacillus*. Although the extraction and purification of the acid are difficult, there is not yet a synthetic process economic enough to replace the fermentation.

$$CH_3COCOOH + NADH_2 \rightarrow CH_3CHOHCOOH + NAD$$

pyruvic acid   lactic acid

Citric acid has important uses in food and pharmacy. It is accumulated by various fungi when they are grown with some poison or nutritional deficiency causing a block in the citric acid cycle at this point. Large quantities are produced commercially by growing *Aspergillus niger* in trays of sterilized molasses medium with added ferrocyanide and phosphate. As much as 90 per cent of the sucrose utilized may be converted to citric acid.

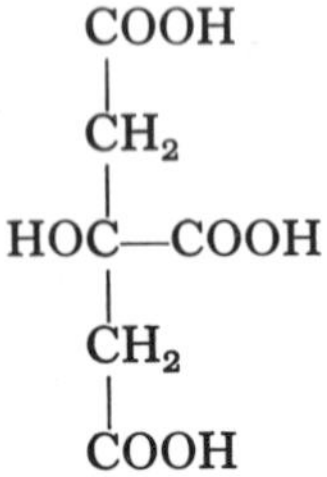

COOH
|
CH$_2$
|
HOC—COOH
|
CH$_2$
|
COOH

citric acid

Gluconic acid which results from a very incomplete oxidation of glucose is known to be produced by a number of micro-organisms. It is used on a wide scale in pharmacy for administering metals, e.g. calcium gluconate. For commercial production *A. niger* is grown in large rotating cylinders on a glucose and mineral salts medium to which an excess of calcium carbonate and a trace of boron are added. Calcium gluconate is recovered from the medium which is drained from the felt of mycelium after about 10 hours. Fresh medium is added to the same mycelium for a semi-continuous process.

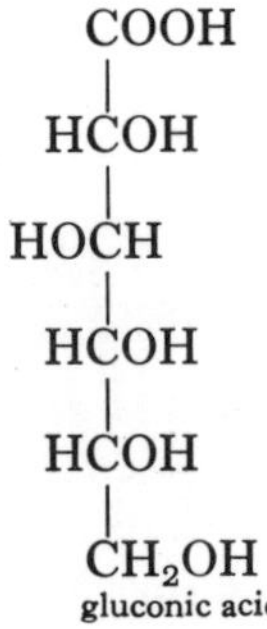

COOH
|
HCOH
|
HOCH
|
HCOH
|
HCOH
|
CH$_2$OH

gluconic acid

Cheese making

This old farm industry is still carried out in some places on a small scale, though standard products are obtained from modern factories. Fresh milk may be fermented by its natural flora, the main organisms of which are *Streptococcus lactis* and a yeast-like organism, *Oidium lactis*. These act on lactose to produce lactic acid which quickly lowers the pH sufficiently to coagulate the casein and form a curd which holds the fat globules. The whey containing some residual lactose is drained away. A small amount of the fresh product may be used as cream cheese, but to form hard cheese the curd is cut and pressed to reduce the water content. Salt is added and the hard curd is made into large cheeses. These are stored under special conditions to control the ripening which is brought about by the continued, slow growth of many micro-organisms.

In modern cheese factories the milk is first pasteurized and then inoculated with pure cultures of *S. lactis* called cheese starters. Sometimes infection of the starter cultures with bacteriophage causes great concern. More recently, cheese makers have been troubled by levels of antibiotics in milk, coming from cows treated for udder infections, sufficient to prevent the growth and development of the starter organisms.

Silage

Silage is made by building large stacks or filling pits with freshly-cut green fodder compressed in layers, each sprinkled with prepared salt and sometimes also with molasses. The mass quickly ferments and heats, at first due to growth mainly of species of *Escherichia* and *Aerobacter* which are followed by many anaerobic organisms. Acetic, lactic, butyric and propionic acids develop and form esters giving the mixture its strong characteristic smell, but also forming flavours which cattle like. After three or four weeks the heated fermenting mass cools down and a stable, digestible foodstuff results.

ANTIBIOTICS

In the years since World War II an industry worth hundreds of millions of pounds has been developed for extracting the metabolites which some micro-organisms produce and which, in great dilution, are effective in halting or killing harmful parasites. Most of the antibiotics are bacterio- or fungi-static, stopping the growth of organisms without actually killing them, but by their use bacterial diseases have largely been conquered. Only a few of these modern drugs are completely without harmful effect on the host, but even those which show some degree of toxicity are exceedingly useful when the slight harmful effect they have is measured against serious disease or even death. Some are effective against many different organisms, when they are said to be broad-spectrum antibiotics, but others are able to act only on certain types of diseases.

All the antibiotics are complex substances but thorough investigation has revealed their chemical structure. Though these are diverse the compounds can be placed in three distinct groups (Table 6.1):

1. antibiotics derived from amino acids;
2. antibiotics derived from sugars;
3. antibiotics derived from acetate or propionate units.

About thirty different compounds are being widely used while a continuous search goes on for more and possibly better substances. Many different isolates of fungi and bacteria are examined annually for production of antibiotics by screening with the agar diffusion technique. For this test petri dishes of agar seeded with a pathogen such as *Staphylococcus aureus*, or some other test organism, are prepared and a number of discs are cut out from the agar to leave rows of holes. A piece from a colony of each organism to be tested, or else an extract from it, is placed in each hole. A variation of the method is to apply the solution containing possible antibiotics on a small disc of filter paper laid on the surface of a prepared plate, or else to place it inside a metal ring. If the material in the hole has any antibiotic activity the growth of the pathogen in the surrounding agar into which it diffuses will be halted leaving a clear halo round the hole. Wherever there is no antibiotic effect the pathogenic bacteria develop into small colonies in the agar making a cloud of spots. The width of clear ring round a hole gives a measure of the degree of effectiveness of the substance (Fig. 6.2). After first selection of a compound by this method its

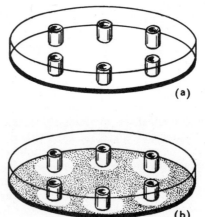

(a)

(b)

Fig. 6.2   Diagram illustrating the agar diffusion test.

toxicity must be tested and its chemical nature determined in order to find out if it is really new and distinct from others already discovered.

Table 6.1   Examples of Antibiotic spectra

Organisms and diseases controlled			Antibiotic derived from												
Type	Species	Main diseases	chloramphenicol	amino acid			sugar			acetate and propionate					
				penicillin G	bacitracin	viomycin	streptomycin	neomycin	paranomycin	tetracyclines	griseofulvin	erythromycin	fumagillin	nystatin	puromycin
Rickettsias	*Rickettsia prowazekii*	epidemic typhus	1							+					
Gram-positive	*Staphylococcus aureus*	pyogenic infection	+	+	+			+		+		+			
	Diplococcus pneumoniae	pneumonia		+	1					+		+			
	Streptococcus pyogenes	scarlet fever		+	1			1				+			
	Corynebacterium diphtheriae	diphtheria		+	1										
	Clostridium tetani	tetanus		+	1										
Acid-fast	*Mycobacterium tuberculosis*	tuberculosis				+	+								
Gram-negative	*Salmonella typhi*	typhoid fever	+							+					
	Klebsiella pneumoniae	pneumonia	+				+	1		+					
	Bordetella pertussis	whooping cough	+				+	1		+					
	Neisseria gonorrhoeae	gonorrhoea	+	+						+		+			
Spirochaetes	*Treponema pallidum*	syphilis	+	+						+					
Fungi	*Trichophyton spp.* *Microsporum spp.*	dermatophytic infection									+				
	Mucor spp.	systemic mycoses									+			+	
Protozoa	*Entamoeba histolytica*	amoebic dysentery carcinoma							+				+		+ +

+ = good control   1 = some control

Commercial production

Antibiotics are produced commercially by pure culture of the selected organism on a very large scale. Vessels of up to 30,000 gallons are filled with sterile medium and inoculated with 1 per cent of seed culture. The mixture is agitated and aerated under the right temperature conditions till growth reaches a stage favourable for reaping. Antibiotic production is not necessarily parallel with growth so the point for reaping must be determined by testing. After the cultures have been filtered or centrifuged to separate the organisms, the antibiotic is extracted from the spent medium by using solvents, adsorbents, ion-exchange materials, or by precipitation. Often combinations of methods are used (Plate 8C).

Examples of antibiotics

1. *Derived from amino acids*

Chloramphenicol has a relatively simple chemical structure and is the only antibiotic which can be synthesized more cheaply than it can be prepared from the living organism. It was first found in cultures of *Streptomyces venezuelae* and soon after was obtained also from *S. lavendulae*. It is a wide-spectrum compound active against a range of both Gram-positive and Gram-negative bacteria and with some activity against *Rickettsias*. It has been a good subject for studying the effects of variations in chemical structure on biological activity. Research workers have prepared a series of analogues, which are compounds differing from the natural one in certain small details of the molecule. None, however, has proved as effective as the original antibiotic. As chloramphenicol is rapidly and efficiently absorbed through the intestine it can be given as pills and has proved particularly effective in the treatment of typhoid fever. Its mode of action is to interfere with protein synthesis in the susceptible cell by modifying the nature of its RNA.

Penicillin, the story of which is widely known, was the first spectacularly successful antibiotic, halting all staphylococcal infections, active against a wide range of Gram-positive organisms and yet at the same time being virtually non-toxic to the host. It is still the most important antibiotic. Early preparations were unstable and results with them were inconsistent till it was discovered that different types of penicillin were formed under different conditions. Six different forms were eventually recognized, and although total synthesis proved difficult it was accomplished. Of the analogues which have been prepared and tested some have useful extra properties and are more stable than the main natural form, penicillin G. This was the substance prepared in America by the large-scale culture of *Penicillium notatum* on corn steep liquor. In England where the same mould was grown on a synthetic medium penicillin F was obtained. Modern prac-

Plate 5 (**A**) Tobacco mosaic disease: middle row of plants infected, side rows healthy. (**B**) Angular leaf spot of tobacco: early infection of seedling leaves by *Pseudomonas angulata*. (By courtesy of Cawthron Institute, Nelson, New Zealand.)

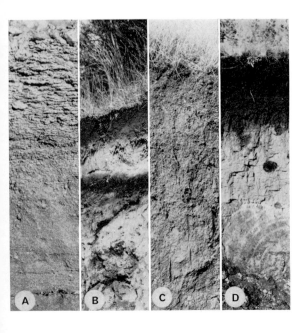

Plate 6 Soil profiles. **(A)** Taylor dry valley, Antarctica; an arctic type of soil. **(B)** Te Kopuru sand, New Zealand; a podzol. **(C)** Kaikoura silt loam, New Zealand. **(D)** Chernozem in Russia. (By courtesy of New Zealand Soil Bureau.) **(E)** A portion of *Botrytis cinerea* mycelium stained with fluorescein-iso-thiocyanate labelled γ-globulin from the serum of a rabbit inoculated with *B. cinerea*. **(F)** Mycelium of *Mycosphaerella melonis*, treated with *B. cinerea* antiserum as in (E). The fluorescence of the mycelium is visible due to staining, but no coating with fluorescent antibody can be seen at the hyphal surface, as shown in (E). (From Preece, T. F. and Cooper, Dorothy, *Trans. Br. mycol. Soc.*, **52**, 104 (1969), Pl. 7, Figs. 2 and 4.)

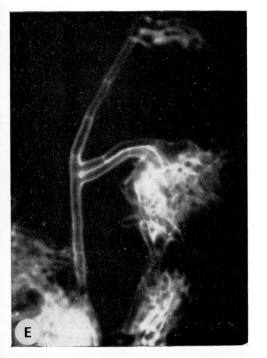

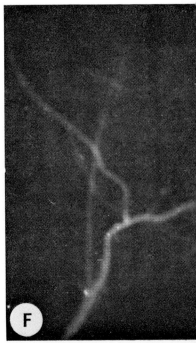

tice is to use a high-yielding strain of *P. chrysogenum* and to add phenyl-acetic acid derivatives to the medium, which induces preferential formation of penicillin G. Although a continuous culture apparatus would seem to offer great advantages for large-scale production, no satisfactory method has yet been worked out to replace the cultivation of the fungus in bulk batches.

Resistant strains of disease organisms which produce a penicillinase and so destroy the drug have arisen, on account of which penicillin is used more carefully than in the years immediately after its discovery. By administering it in conjunction with another antibiotic there is less likelihood of selecting resistant strains. The mode of action of penicillin is to prevent the incorporation of amino groups into the bacterial wall substance which then has no capacity to bind together into a solid structure. The naked protoplasts which result from cell division soon disappear.

Bacitracin is a polypeptide antibiotic isolated from cultures of *Bacillus licheniformis* and also of *B. subtilis*. Various forms have high activity against Gram-positive infections, but toxicity to kidney tissue limits their usefulness. As bacitracin is not rapidly absorbed into the body it is used for treatment of infections of the skin and mucous membranes. The polypeptide antibiotics generally are surface active and damage the cytoplasmic membranes which become permeable and lose cell substances.

Viomycin, obtained from cultures of *Streptomyces puniceus* and *S. floridae*, is a cyclic polypeptide with activity against *Mycobacterium tuberculosis* and is useful in treating infections which show resistance to streptomycin.

2. Derived from sugars

Streptomycin, which is a quite different type of chemical compound from penicillin is possibly the next most important antibiotic because it is active against the organism of tuberculosis which withstands most other drugs. It is produced by cultures of *Streptomyces griseus*. Its mode of action is not fully understood but it interferes with the pathogen's respiratory processes and prevents synthesis of new membranes. It is not completely non-toxic as it may affect the eighth cranial nerve impairing hearing and balance. As bacteria readily develop resistance to this and related antibiotics they are used in combinations including other therapeutic agents.

Neomycin from *S. fradiae* is a compound somewhat similar to streptomycin. **Paranomycin** from *S. rimosus* is important because it is active against *Entamoeba histolytica* and so will cure amoebic dysentery.

3. Derived from acetate or propionate units

The **tetracyclines** are a group of antibiotics of similar structure with broad spectra of activity. They are found among the metabolic products of

S. aureofaciens and *S. rimosus* and as they are compounds of low toxicity they are proving very useful. Chlortetracycline is widely known under the name *aureomycin*. Apart from their use in medicine, tetracyclines are being added to prevent food spoilage especially in pies and other cooked foods, and for fish. Their application in this way should be carefully controlled as there is always a danger that resistant organisms will be selected by widespread use, and some consumers of treated food may show allergic reactions. Because they stimulate the growth of young animals an important place for them has been found in animal nutrition, and they are being added to many stock foods. The increase in animal growth may follow from a reduction in the numbers of unimportant organisms in the gut with a consequent increase in those which are known to synthesize B-group vitamins. A recently reported use for chlortetracycline is in the cultured pearl industry in Japan where it is used successfully to prevent infection which sometimes follows after the seed has been introduced into the living oysters. The mode of action of the tetracyclines is to interfere with protein synthesis inside the susceptible cells.

Griseofulvin, which was first recovered from the mycelium of *Penicillium griseofulvum*, has been found to be formed by many other *Penicillium* species. It has antifungal properties, acting on hyphae by interfering with wall formation so that the tips curl and cease to grow. When administered orally it is absorbed into the body where it accumulates in the keratinized tissues of the epidermis and hair and thus is especially effective against the fungal skin infections such as ring-worm and athlete's foot. It has been used on plants which will absorb it from a foliar spray and translocate it through the tissues so that it appears to be a possible systemic fungicide. Its full usefulness has yet to be demonstrated as it is still too expensive for ordinary crop protection. In general, antibiotics are too costly for treating individual plants which have little value in comparison with animals.

Erythromycin, a cyclic compound obtained from *Streptomyces erythreus*, is similar in effect to penicillin but is not affected by penicillinase. As it also shows low toxicity it is an important additional antibiotic.

Fumagillin, a complex compound formed by *Aspergillus fumigatus*, is an important agent against amoebic dysentery. Closely related compounds such as **nystatin** from *S. noursei* have antifungal properties.

Puromycin, obtained from *S. alboniger*, is a recent antibiotic which has shown anti-tumour activity. Its analogues are being energetically investigated.

OTHER MICROBIAL PRODUCTS

Dextrans

Many micro-organisms produce extracellular polysaccharides some of which are useful in pharmacy. Dextrans produced from *Leuconostoc mesenteroides* have been used as blood plasma extenders and possible uses may be found for other similar products.

Vitamins

These are often lacking in cheap foodstuffs which can, however, be improved if the necessary compounds are added. Many micro-organisms secrete small quantities of B-group vitamins, the level of which in the final culture medium may be increased by adjusting its original composition.

Riboflavin is extracted on a large scale from aerated, submerged cultures of the yeast *Ashbya gossypii* grown on corn steep liquor with certain additives. Production has reached the high level of about 180 tons per annum. Riboflavin is an important additive for both human and animal food.

Cobamides, Vitamin B$_{12}$, are probably produced only by micro-organisms, higher animals normally depending on the bacteria of the gut to provide what they need. Commercial production has been carried out using cultures of either *Streptomyces olivaceus* or *Bacillus megaterium* grown on a medium containing carbohydrate and a rich organic nitrogen source (Plate 4B). Most of the vitamin remains in the living cells which must be extracted when the crop is reaped. Cobamides have been found to be present in dried sewage sludge from which the vitamin is extracted commercially in Milwaukee.

Gibberellins

These plant hormones are produced abundantly by the fungus *Gibberella fujikuroi* which causes a disease of rice accompanied by abnormal elongation. Both cell division and extension are increased in plant apices by treatment with less than one part per million of the active substance. This has been used to accelerate the growth of several horticultural crops and serves as a valuable stimulant in malt making. In the future a much wider use may be found for these compounds which are still under investigation.

Enzymes

Useful enzymes are produced commercially from a number of micro-organisms. Cultures of *Aspergillus niger* and *A. oryzae* on trays of moist, sterile bran yield the well-known Japanese **amylase**. *Bacillus subtilis* has also been used to produce amylase, which it will do abundantly in a starch-free medium. The enzyme secreted by these micro-organisms contains two main kinds of starch-splitting component. The first, called α-amylase, attacks both straight and branched chain polymers to produce short chain compounds. The second, called β-amylase, hydrolyses these smaller units or long straight chains to disaccharide. **Invertase**, which has a number of industrial uses, is extracted from *Saccharomyces cerevisiae*. It is an example of a specific enzyme (p. 46) which hydrolyses, or inverts, sucrose to a mixture of glucose and fructose.

Pectinase enzymes, which dissolve the pectic middle lamellae of cell walls so causing tissues to disintegrate, are important in all soft rot plant parasites and saprophytes. The process of ***retting*** depends on the activity of two kinds of such organisms according to whether it is carried out aerobically or anaerobically. Where the flax or other fibre to be retted is spread out above ground it is subject to frequent wetting and drying. Here the separation of the fibres, called dew retting, is brought about by a number of organisms including *B. subtilis* and *B. macerans* together with species of *Rhizopus* and *Mucor*. Anaerobic retting which may be carried out in large tanks, and which was formerly worked by leaving the material in peaty ponds, depends mainly on the growth of *Clostridium* species. Pectinase is used on a considerable scale in the food industry to clarify fruit juices. Proteolytic enzymes from bacterial cultures find important use in the 'biological' washing powders.

MICRO-ORGANISMS IN CHEMICAL SYNTHESES

Often compounds which are first discovered and originally manufactured by biological methods are subsequently produced more cheaply by straight chemical synthesis. Pure ethanol which once could be obtained only from fermentation products is now made more economically by chemical methods. The synthesis of some of the newer more complex compounds involves many distinct steps, for some of which a biological method is cheaper and easier than a purely chemical operation. For this reason some commercial products are manufactured partly by chemical processes and partly by the aid of micro-organisms.

Vitamin C

Synthesized on a very large scale for fortifying foodstuffs, vitamin C is also used as an anti-oxidant in some food preparations. The starting material is glucose which is first reduced electrolytically to sorbitol. The next stage, the conversion of sorbitol to sorbose, is carried out by culturing *Acetobacter suboxydans* on the material. Then by further chemical steps sorbose is converted to ascorbic acid (Fig. 6.3).

Steroid formation

Several important biological compounds are complex steroids which are not easily synthesized. A number of important reactions in industrial pro-

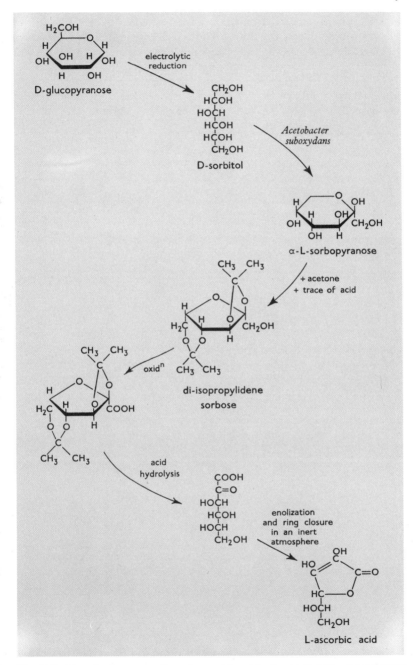

Fig. 6.3 Steps in the preparation of ascorbic acid, vitamin C, using *Acetobacter suboxydans*.

cesses involving steroid chemistry are brought about by using a selected organism under special conditions. The fungus *Cunninghamella blakesleeana* is used, for example, to bring about a hydroxylation and so convert cortexolone to cortisone, an important modern drug.

In this field of industrial activity rapid progress is following the combined efforts of microbiologists and chemists who are working out how to use individual bacteria and fungi for some difficult specific reactions.

PART III

DIVERSITY OF FUNGI IN RELATION TO ENVIRONMENT

7

Chytridiomycetes, Oomycetes and Zygomycetes

The lower classes of true fungi have a certain amount in common though they are undoubtedly sufficiently distinct to justify separation. Formerly they were treated together under the heading Phycomycetes, though this was perhaps more for convenience than from any recently upheld belief in their close relationship. The older name implied a connection with algae, but as far as this may be entertained in the light of present-day knowledge it could be suggested as a possibility only for the Saprolegniales. On the other hand a connection with the Protozoa seems equally likely. The first two classes, grouped together by Dr. Ainsworth as the sub-division Mastigomycotina, include the fungi which typically produce motile cells. Many of them are either aquatic or favoured by damp conditions. The purely terrestrial Zygomycetes include the well-known pin moulds with wide-diameter coenocytic hyphae which may reach a high degree of specialization, and which are clearly a distinct group.

CHYTRIDIOMYCETES

The Chytridiomycetes are characterized by motile cells with a single posterior whiplash flagellum. They include the following three orders.

Chytridiales

The Chytridiales, or chytrids as they are often called, are regarded as the simplest of the true fungi. The species are typically aquatic though some live in damp soil. They may grow as saprophytes, or as parasites on algae or in the roots of higher plants. The thallus of these fungi may be a simple unicell or a small coenocyte with a few simple branches. Asexual reproduction is by uninucleate zoospores while sexual reproduction, in the simplest cases, is by equal motile gametes which resemble zoospores (Fig. 7.1).

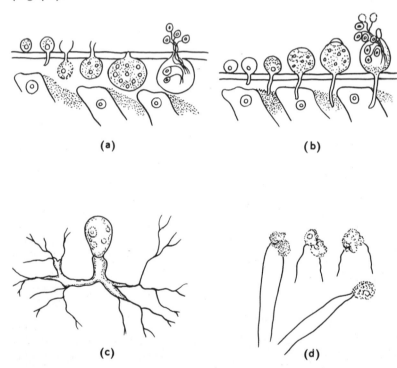

(a)　　　　　　　　　　　(b)

(c)　　　　　　　　　　　(d)

Fig. 7.1 Examples of the Chytridiales : (a) *Olpidium*, encysted zoospore on wall of *Spirogyra* cell, and stages of development to sporangium discharging zoospores ; (b) *Chytridium*, series from encysted zoospore to dehiscence of mature sporangium by an operculum and shedding of zoospores ; (c) young thallus of *Asterophlyctis* ; (d) sexual reproduction in *Olpidium trifolii*, fusion of isogametes. (After Sparrow, F. J., 1960, *Aquatic Phycomycetes*, University of Michigan Press, Ann Arbor.)

Synchytrium endobioticum, the parasite causing wart disease of potatoes (Fig. 5.10), is an example of a simple chytrid with a life history of the type in which equal motile cells may behave either as zoospores or as gametes according to the external conditions. Microscopic haploid motile cells are shed from an infected host into the soil. Under wet conditions these behave as zoospores. They swim in soil moisture and may infect an epidermal cell of a potato tuber, growing within the host into an enlarged cell called a prosorus. At the same time the surrounding tuber cells are stimulated to grow into a wart. Within the wart the prosorus divides to form a group, or sorus, of sporangia in each of which 200 or 300 motile cells are formed. If these are liberated under wet conditions they behave as zoospores and repeat the same cycle, but if conditions are drier they behave as gametes, fusing in pairs. The zygotes may penetrate epidermal cells of tubers in the same way as zoospores, but induce the formation of the typical large, rough wart. In the sporangia developed from a zygote meiosis is presumed to occur, and haploid motile cells are again liberated. Such a life history shows a very simple stage in the development of sex, as the environment appears to control whether the motile cells function as gametes or as zoospores. The species of *Olpidium* have a similar life history to that of *Synchytrium*, but produce single sporangia. Some species infect the roots of many different higher plants without causing serious disease, but may be important because the motile cells are able to carry virus particles from one host to another.

Blastocladiales

Allomyces, a genus of the Blastocladiales, is a more highly developed type in the same group. The species of *Allomyces* show a regular alternation of generations. A tiny, hyphal, branched haploid gametothallus produces motile gametes of two kinds differing in size and colour. The orange male gametes are about half the size of the colourless female ones. The zygotes formed from the fusion of two sex cells grow into diploid sporothalli which are very similar to the gametothalli but they bear two kinds of sporangia. One liberates diploid zoospores which grow into further diploid sporothalli. The other is a thick-walled resting sporangium in which meiosis is presumed to occur because it liberates haploid zoospores from which further gametothalli develop. Although this life history shows a more rigid establishment of sexual reproduction than the life histories of simpler genera, the pattern is not completely unalterable. Some strains producing gametothalli which are either mainly male or mainly female have been subjected to nutritional tests. By use of different synthetic media it has been possible to induce a high degree of maleness, so that to some extent even in these fungi external conditions may influence sex.

Blastocladiella of the same order includes species which may have three or even four types of thalli, each of which produces swarm cells of a definite kind (Fig. 7.2). These may be zoospores, or male or female gametes. Studies in morphogenesis have shown that carbon dioxide fixation, which may be stimulated by light, is important in influencing the course of development of these different forms.

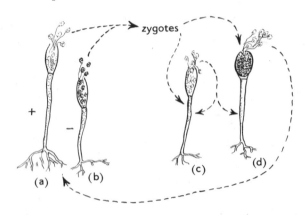

Fig. 7.2 Diagram of the life cycle of *Blastocladiella variabilis*. (a and b) Gametangial plants which produce morphologically similar gametes, orange coloured from one plant, colourless from another. Zygotes develop into sporangial plants which are either (c) bearing zoospores which grow into similar zoosporangial plants or (d) sporangial plants bearing thick-walled sporangia. These, on germination, form zoospores which grow into a new generation of gametangial plants. (After Sparrow, F. J., 1960, *Aquatic Phycomycetes*, University of Michigan Press, Ann Arbor.)

Monoblepharidales

A small group of aquatic fungi of which *Monoblepharis* is an example is thought to represent the culmination of the chytrid group. The thallus, which consists of characteristically highly-vacuolated hyphae, may form sporangia which liberate typical zoospores each capable of germinating into a new thallus. The same thallus may produce sex organs. The female gametangia, or oogonia, each contain a sessile egg cell or oosphere. The smaller male organs, the antheridia, liberate a number of antherozoids, one of which may fuse with the oosphere to form a zygote. This emerges from the oogonium and secretes a thick wall so forming an oospore.

OOMYCETES

In the Oomycetes asexual reproduction is typically by zoospores of characteristic type, each with a tinsel flagellum directed forwards and a whiplash backwards (Plate 1). Fertilization of oospheres follows the fusion of gametangia and oospores are formed. The hyphal wall in fungi of this group has been found to consist mainly of cellulose with some hemicellulose and a skeletal framework of chitin. The species range from comparatively simple aquatic fungi to highly specialized, terrestrial, obligate parasites, including some of great economic importance.

Saprolegnia

This common water mould, an example of a simple Oomycete, is frequently found growing in ponds on organic remains such as dead insects. A coenocytic mycelium of narrow feeding hyphae spreads through the

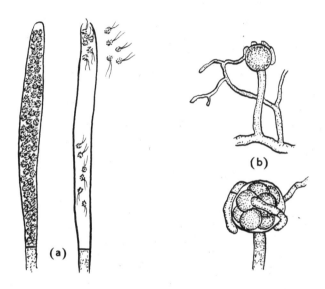

Fig. 7.3 *Saprolegnia*. (a) Zoosporangia. (b) Gametangia (after Smith, G. M., 1938, *Cryptogamic Botany*, I, McGraw-Hill, New York and Maidenhead).

substrate from the surface of which arises a fur of thicker branching vegetative hyphae. Zoosporangia are formed at hyphal tips which are cut off by crosswalls (Fig. 7.3a). The contents of each divide to form many biflagellate zoospores each of which, after swimming in the water, may **encyst** by attaching itself to some substrate, withdrawing its flagella and forming a delicate wall.

Instead of germinating by a germ tube to form a hypha, as the zoospores of closely related fungi do, the encysted zoospores of *Saprolegnia* form a second generation of zoospores which are kidney-shaped with the two flagella arising at the side. The species of fungi which show two successive types of zoospores are said to be ***diplanetic*** in comparison with ***monoplanetic*** species which have only one kind. When the second zoospore encysts it may germinate to give rise to a new hyphal system.

The same mycelium which bears zoospores develops oogonia containing several oospheres, and smaller antheridia. When the gametangia (Fig. 7.3b) fuse the antheridium pushes out a fertilization tube which penetrates the wall of the oogonium, and through this tube antheridial contents reach the oospheres which, after fertilization, develop into thick-walled oospores. In the closely related water mould *Achlya* there are dioecious species in which complex hormone systems have been demonstrated. A female thallus liberates a hormone which induces the formation of antheridia on neighbouring male thalli. The antheridial branches then produce a hormone which stimulates oogonial formation on the female plants. These then produce a third hormone which attracts the antheridia to the oogonia. After contact further hormones stimulate maturation of the oogonia.

Pythium

This genus includes many well-known terrestrial Oomycetes of damp habitats, several of which are facultative parasites causing damping-off of seedlings or soft-rotting of plant tissues. The mycelium is made up, typically, of rather slender coenocytic hyphae which spread through soil or plant tissues. In asexual reproduction, which usually occurs freely, the globose or filamentous sporangia formed on the tips or in the middle of some of the hyphae (Fig. 7.4b) normally germinate in a special manner. A short narrow tube grows out from the sporangium, the contents of which flow through the tube to form a bubble-like vesicle with a very slender wall. Zoospores are formed immediately and may be seen moving rapidly within the vesicle before it bursts (Fig. 7.4c). After a period of swimming in the surrounding moisture the zoospores come to rest, encyst and germinate to form a new mycelium. *P. ultimum*, a fairly common species, is exceptional in having sporangia which germinate directly to form a hyphal growth.

Sexual reproduction occurs on the mycelium at any time, antheridia and oogonia being formed together, usually on the same hypha. The oogonium is a large, terminal globose structure with a smooth or spiny wall in which a single oosphere develops surrounded by an envelope of periplasm. One or more antheridial branches grow out below the oogonium and at the tip of each an antheridium develops as a small elongated or club-shaped structure. The tip of it fuses with the oogonial wall which is penetrated by a short fertilization tube. One functional male nucleus passes with the antheridial contents into the oosphere where fusion takes place. The zygote develops into a smooth thick-walled ***oospore*** which remains dormant for a variable period after being shed by decay of the old oogonium (Fig. 7.4a). When it germinates the germ tube pierces the oogonial wall and develops into a vesicle which may grow into a new mycelium or it may form a sporangium at once.

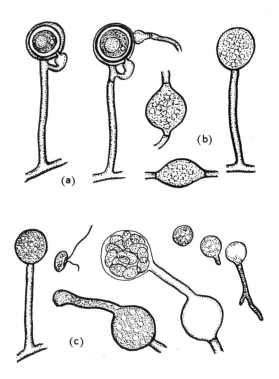

Fig. 7.4   (a) *Pythium ultimum* : sexual reproduction, fusion of gametangia and formation of oospores. (b) *P. ultimum* : terminal and intercalary sporangia. (c) *P. hypogynum* : terminal sporangium, formation of vesicle and zoospores, free zoospore and germination of encysted zoospore. (After Middleton, J. T., 1943, *Mem. Torrey bot. Club*, **20**, 1.)

Diploid thallus

It is of especial interest that nuclear divisions with some features of meiosis have been shown to occur in the gametangia of *P. debaryanum*. In this species the vegetative mycelium thus appears to be diploid and only the gametes are haploid, but it iş not known whether this is general for the group.

Phytophthora

This genus is closely related to *Pythium* and has similar reproductive structures except that sporangia are borne on special branching sporangiophores. It includes some virulent plant pathogens of which the best known is *Phytophthora infestans*, the potato blight organism. The mycelium of this species consists of a branching system of moderately thick coenocytic hyphae which ramify through the host tissues in the intercellular spaces, giving off branched haustoria which invaginate the protoplasm of the living cells from which they draw nutriment. Under warm, humid conditions slender, branching sporangiophores which are distinct from the somatic hyphae are formed, often in great abundance, extending through stomata or lenticels or arising from broken surfaces. A succession of small ovoid sporangia is shed from the tips of the indefinitely branched sporangiophores (Fig. 7.5, Plate 2). These are blown or splashed with raindrops on to

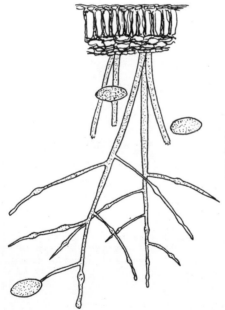

Fig. 7.5 *Phytophthora infestans* sporangiophores growing from the underside of a diseased potato leaf.

other plants where they may germinate in two ways. At low temperatures the contents of the sporangium divide to form a number of biflagellate zoospores which are released to swim for a while in the surface moisture. Each may encyst, then germinate to form a special short hypha, an **appressorium**, which adheres closely to the leaf surface. From the underside of this structure a narrow, peg-like, infection hypha forces its way down through the epidermis into the living cells below to start a new infection. At higher temperatures zoospores are not formed. Instead the sporangium itself grows directly into a new hypha which may enter the leaf tissues through a stoma. The sporangia of other species of *Phytophthora* behave similarly (Fig. 7.6). This suggests how conidia have arisen, at least in the higher Oomycetes, where they are small single-celled sporangia.

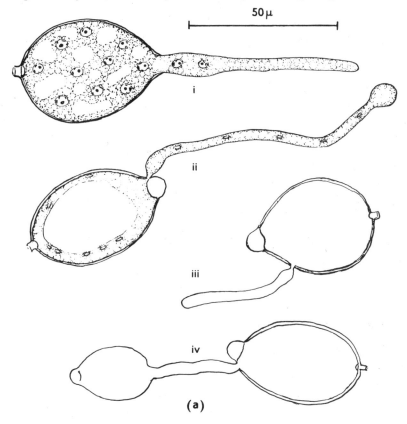

Fig. 7.6   (a) direct germination of sporangia of *Phytophthora cactorum.*

Sexual reproduction in *P. infestans* is not often seen, but when it occurs gametangia are formed at the ends of hyphae. As an oogonium forms it grows through the middle of a developing antheridium which is

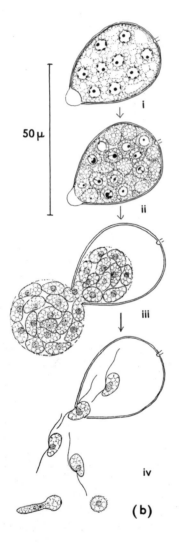

Fig. 7.6 (b) indirect germination of sporangia of *Phytophthora cactorum*.
((a) and (b) after original drawings by Miss E. Blackwell.)

then left forming a collar round the oogonial base. Fertilization is presumed to take place before the thick-walled oospore is developed within the oogonium. When this germinates it may form a sporangium immediately or else it may give rise to a new hyphal growth. Other species and strains of *Phytophthora* are also of economic importance, e.g. *P. cactorum* causing foot rot of apples and pears, and *P. parasitica* var. *nicotianae* causing basal stem rot of tobacco (Plate 8A).

Heterothallism

Many fungi require two different strains of the species to grow together before sexual reproduction occurs. Each strain may produce both male and female organs but it may be, nevertheless, self-sterile, requiring some factor from the opposite strain before fertilization can occur. This may be some element of nutrition or some hormone since in certain cases of self-sterility substances diffusing from one strain to another may be sufficient to induce self-fertilization in each. In other cases only cross-fertilization is possible and the factor, whether it concerns nutrition or not, is plainly genetic.

P. infestans exists in strains which are largely, but not completely, self-sterile. In temperate countries generally, where the fungus occurs mainly on cultivated potatoes and occasionally on tomatoes, it reproduces vigorously by asexual spores but oospores are not seen. Only one strain appears to be represented, but oospores are formed exceptionally in culture on rich media by the single strain. In Central America where the fungus occurs on a number of wild species of *Solanum* as well as on cultivated plants different strains are present and sexual reproduction occurs commonly by cross-fertilization of gametangia of any two compatible strains. The nutrition of the strain and its occurrence on different hosts have an influence on its sexual compatibility.

Heterothallism, is a condition which resembles genetically controlled incompatibility. The condition was first discovered in the Zygomycetes, many of which produce identical gametangia. For many species mycelia grown from a single spore are always self-sterile, but when two opposite strains named plus and minus meet, their gametangia fuse together in pairs. Among the higher Basidiomycetes where no sex organs are formed and vegetative fusion results in dikaryotomy, many species are heterothallic with the plus and minus strains morphologically identical but physiologically different. That heterothallism is controlled genetically is shown by growing haploid spores formed after a meiosis separately. Bipolar heterothallic species give equal numbers of plus and minus strains.

Simple or bipolar heterothallism concerns two strains where the fusion behaviour is governed by a single pair of genes, but multiple allelomorphic heterothallism is known for many species, especially among the Homobasidiomycetidae. Tetrapolar heterothallism controlled by two allellomorphic pairs of genes results in four strains of haplonts each with a distinct mating behaviour, e.g. if the genes for mating behaviour in the diplont are represented by AAaa, BBbb then the four possible haploid strains are AB, Ab, aB, ab. Other more complex systems are known.

Homothallism

This condition, in contrast to that described above, is found in species of which the diploid or dikaryotic stage of the fungus results from the growth of a single haploid stage or haplont.

Peronospora

The numerous species of this genus are obligate parasites causing downy mildews on many kinds of plants. *P. parasitica* which occurs on crucifers is an example. The intercellular mycelium which extends in leaves or stems consists of hyphae of irregular thickness. Branched haustoria arising from these hyphae are pushed into the living cells. The sporangiophores which are formed on the leaf surfaces are much branched and quite distinct from the internal hyphae. Unlike those of *Phytophthora* they are repeatedly dichotomously branched and produce a number of sporangia simultaneously, the production terminating the development of the branch (Fig. 7.7). Each single-celled 'sporangium' always germinates by a germ

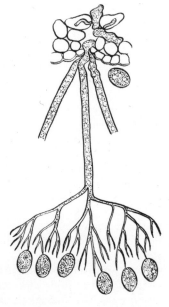

Fig. 7.7 Conidiophores of *Peronospora parasitica* causing downy mildew on *Cheiranthus* (wallflower) ; details of one conidiophore only, haustoria in host cells.

tube. Zoospores are not formed in this genus and the sporangia are usually called conidia. Sex organs which are found in only a few strains of *Peronospora parasitica* are formed buried in the host tissues where thick-walled oospores may remain dormant till the host tissues decay. When an oospore germinates it usually forms a hypha but may produce a sporangiophore.

Albugo

The species of *Albugo* are also obligate parasites which attack many crop and ornamental plants as well as some weeds, causing the white blister rusts. *A. candida* which attacks various crucifers is often seen in late summer. The somatic hyphae which grow in the intercellular spaces are somewhat irregular and give rise to rounded haustoria which protrude into the host cells. Short club-shaped sporangiophores are formed in dense

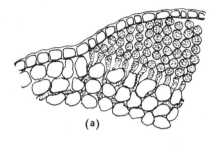

(a)

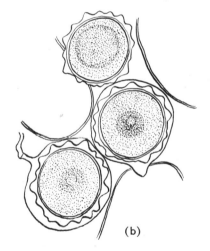

(b)

Fig. 7.8 *Albugo candida* causing white blister rust on radish stem : (a) part of sorus of sporangia ; (b) oospores in the pith.

groups under the epidermis. From the tip of each, a chain of successive sporangia is cut off till finally the epidermis is raised in a blister which bursts exposing a white mass of colourless sporangia (Fig. 7.8). These germinate by liberating a number of zoospores. Sexual reproduction follows the usual pattern for the group and the thick-walled, warty oospores are formed within the host tissues. When the oospore germinates it always produces 40–60 zoospores which are extruded in a vesicle.

Biological races

A. candida or *P. parasitica* collected from different cruciferous hosts shows no morphological variation, yet spores produced on one species of host may be unable to attack a closely related crucifer. The fungi consist of a number of races or *formae speciales* each of which (a forma specialis) is restricted to an individual host species or to a few that are very closely related. This phenomenon of biological specialization is found also in other obligate parasites and is notable among rust fungi where a forma specialis may be able to grow on only one variety of the host.

ZYGOMYCETES

The Zygomycetes are all strictly terrestrial fungi with no motile forms. In asexual reproduction in most species sporangia produce considerable numbers of non-motile sporangiospores. In sexual reproduction two multinucleate gametangia, similar in structure and either equal or differing somewhat in size, fuse together and a compound *zygospore* with many zygote nuclei is formed. The coenocytic hyphae are often of wide diameter (15–20 μ) and show considerable differentiation. Some members of the Zygomycetes are highly specialized.

Rhizopus

Rhizopus stolonifer is a common saprophyte belonging to the Mucorales. Species of the genus *Mucor* are similar and are also well known though they are somewhat less common. The vegetative mycelium of *R. stolonifer* forms clusters of rather narrow rhizoidal hyphae which ramify through the substratum secreting enzymes which digest some of the food substances. Horizontal hyphae run like stolons linking clusters of rhizoidal hyphae. Directly above each cluster of feeding hyphae there is a group of erect sporangiophores, at the tip of each of which a single globose sporangium develops (Fig. 7.9). The dense protoplasm within this which forms the spores lines the wall, while a dome-shaped dividing wall separates the developing spores from the central part of the sporangiophore. When the outer wall finally bursts and the ripe sporangiospores are dispersed by air currents the dividing wall remains as a columella crowning the erect hypha. In *M. hiemalis*, which is a less widespread species, the sporangia are very similar, but when they burst open the sporangiospores are exposed in a droplet of mucilage which prevents them from blowing away. They must be carried by insects or washed by water.

Sexual reproduction

R. stolonifer like many Zygomycetes is heterothallic and requires plus and minus strains to meet before gametangia are formed. When long

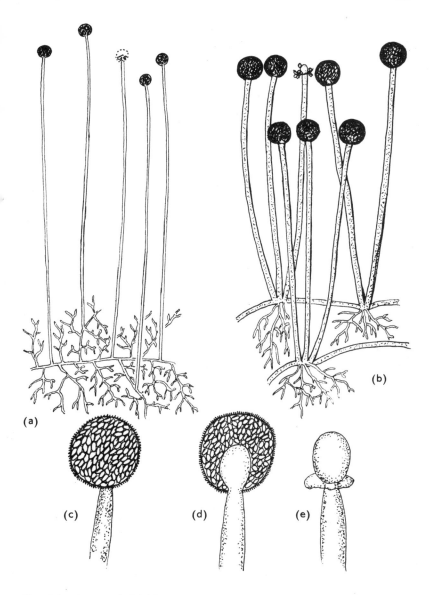

Fig. 7.9   Growth of : (a) *Mucor hiemalis* ; (b) *Rhizopus stolonifer* ; (c) sporangio-phore tip and sporangium of *Mucor* ; (d) same in median sectional view ; (e) sporangiophore tip with columella and remains of sporangial wall after shedding spores.

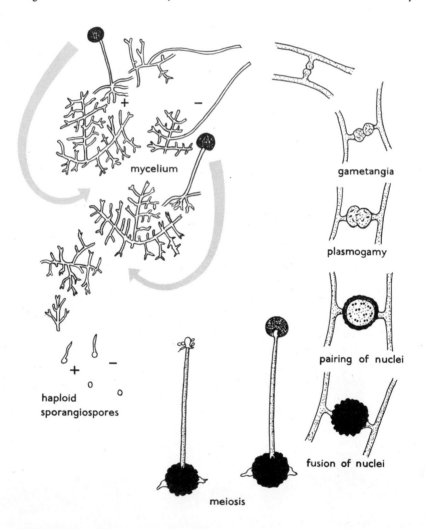

Fig. 7.10 Diagram of life cycle of *Rhizopus*.

running hyphae meet or cross, short branch hyphae of opposite strains
grow together touching at their tips. An equal multinucleate segment cut
off the end of each is the gametangium. The two gametangia fuse, their
contents mingle and the opposite nuclei fuse in pairs. The cell wall of the
fused gametangia enlarges and then thickens to form the rough black
envelope of the resting zygospore (Fig. 7.10). When this germinates it

absorbs water, the thick outer wall splits and the contents grow out to form a sporangiophore. Meiosis occurs in the germinating zygospore so that the sporangiospores formed from it are all haploid. Segregation of mating characters takes place at meiosis so that a single sporangiospore grows into a mycelium of one single strain.

Mating types

Heterothallism (p. 131) is a feature of the Zygomycetes, many species of which require the mating of two strains before sexual reproduction occurs. However, in some species the thallus is self-fertile and sexual reproduction occurs on a mycelium grown from a single sporangiospore.

Pilobolus

Pilobolus is an interesting genus, species of which grow commonly as saprophytes on the dung of herbivorous animals. They have a highly-

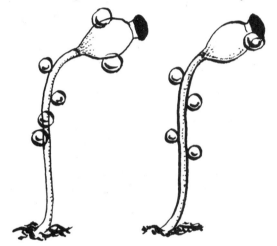

Fig. 7.11   Sporangia of *Pilobolus* (× 20).

specialized spore dispersal mechanism. The large conspicuous sporangiophore, which may reach 2 cm tall, is phototropic. It has a swollen trophocyst at its base and another swollen vesicle, with a bright chrome yellow collar, under the sporangium. When maximum turgor has been reached in the subsporangial vesicle, a process which may be assisted by the secretion of the drops of moisture seen all over its surface, it bursts explosively shooting the whole cap-like sporangium for a distance of 1–2 m while, in examples observed by the writer, the sporangiophore instantly collapses in recoil. If the fungus is illuminated from one side the sporangiophores bend so that they shoot unerringly towards the light (Fig. 7.11). When the sporangium hits surrounding herbage the mucilage base holds it fast. Spores float out from the sporangial mass when it becomes wet. The gametangia are formed on fairly long branch hyphae which meet in a tong-shaped structure.

Endogone

Species of *Endogone*, which also belongs to this class, are found in soil as saprophytes and possibly as parasites. Some species form arbuscular-vesicular mycorrhizas. Older hyphae are characteristically brown and thick walled. The zygospores of some species may be surrounded by a weft of hyphae forming a tuberous, hypogeal fruiting body 1–2 cm in diameter. Other species form similar fructifications which contain only chlamydo-spores. These are the only fruiting bodies known in the Zygomycetes (Fig. 5.6).

Entomophthora

Entomophthora belongs to a large group, the species of which are chiefly parasitic on insects. The hyphae of these fungi do not form a mycelial growth but develop cross walls and break into small hyphal bodies. Asexual reproduction is by small sporangia or sporangiola each of which is shot from the end of the hypha which bears it. As these germinate directly to form a hypha they are also called conidia. Sexual reproduction is by fusion of gametangia which subsequently form zygospores; or **azygospores**, structures of similar form which arise without fusion, may be formed.

TRENDS OF DEVELOPMENT

Within the Chytridiomycetes and Oomycetes there is a gradation from simple aquatic forms to those which are purely terrestrial, and from simple saprophytes to highly specialized obligate parasites. The thallus ranges from unicellular to mycelial, and hyphal systems range from the condition where all hyphae are alike, as in *Pythium*, to complex systems with special-ized haustoria and differentiated sporangiophores. The most primitive asexual reproduction is shown by fungi producing zoospores only, e.g. all the chytrids and the lower Oomycetes. Progression to terrestrial or aerial mode of life where the units of asexual reproduction may develop into either zoospores or conidia, is shown by *Phytophthora* and other genera. In the genera *Peronospora*, *Entomophthora* and others, the sporangia, though plurinucleate, are small and function only as conidia.

Sexual reproduction in the Chytridiomycetes is shown in the lower members in its simplest form, as it is in some algae. Haploid motile cells may behave either as zoospores or as isogametes according to conditions.

Some genera such as *Allomyces* show a size difference in the motile gametes; then *Monoblepharis* shows a clear difference between large, female oospheres and small motile, male gametes. In the Oomycetes the sexual pattern is consistent throughout with fusion of gametangia, gametes being large female oospheres and smaller male antheridial protoplasts. Some Oomycete thalli are self-fertile, others require cross-fertilization between two morphologically similar but compatible strains which are sometimes called plus and minus.

In the case of some genera of these simpler fungi the development of sex organs has been shown in certain species to be influenced or controlled by diffusible substances such as hormones, and the effect of external conditions where important may be due to their influence on the production of such substances. The action of the plus and minus strains on each other has also been shown in some cases to be due to diffusible substances, but in most instances this is not so. In the genus *Pythium*, where a reduction division may take place in the gametangia and only the gametes are haploid, the sexual pattern is assumed to be fixed by the nuclear sequence. In other groups where the main part of the vegetative cycle is believed to be haploid and the diploid stage is limited to the zygote, the life cycle is more flexible. The organism with only one set of genes is subject to mutations the effect of which is immediately expressed.

The Zygomycetes are undoubtedly a specialized group of fungi with their rapidly-growing and often much differentiated, broad coenocytic hyphae. Asexual reproduction is usually by sporangiospores, which may be airborne or may be sticky and require water or possibly insects to spread them, or conidia may be produced. The explosive, light-sensitive mechanism of *Pilobolus* is a highly evolved and efficient method of spreading the spores.

The sexual apparatus is distinctive with fusion of multinucleate gametangia resulting in formation of a large complex zygospore. Species are either self-fertile or heterothallic. In both the Oomycetes and the Zygomycetes sexual reproduction has become less frequent than asexual. It results in the formation of resting spores with the special function of tiding over unfavourable periods while abundant asexual spores serve to spread the fungus under normal conditions of the environment.

8

Ascomycetes

These, together with the Basidiomycetes, are called the higher fungi because they may show considerably more complexity of structure than any of the groups described in the previous chapter. The mycelium often forms fungal 'tissues' (plectenchyma) especially in fructifications which may be large and conspicuous. The sexual fusion of nuclei in Ascomycetes occurs within a characteristic sac-like cell, the ascus. The first division of the fusion nucleus is by meiosis and haploid ascospores, usually eight in number, are formed internally. The majority of species grow as a mycelium but the unicellular yeasts are also members of this group.

ENDOMYCETALES

Saccharomyces

Many species of yeasts occur wild particularly on the surface of fruits and leaves and in soil but the best known is cultivated yeast, *S. cerevisiae*. Single yeast cells are small, 5–10 μ in diameter, and ovoid in shape. Each has a more or less central vacuole capped by a small nucleus. Mitochondria are present and a few storage granules. Growth is by budding. Daughter cells may bud while still attached to the parent so that short chains of cells may hang together for a time (Fig. 8.1). Asexual reproduction by budding may continue rapidly with vigorous aerobic respiration or under anaerobic conditions cells may grow slowly, or simply respire without budding. Some other yeasts in which the cells divide transversely into equal daughter cells instead of growing by budding are called fission yeasts.

Sexual reproduction in yeasts

Some species and strains of yeasts produce asci frequently though in others the sexual stages are rarely seen. In *S. cerevisiae* the ordinary budding cells may be haploid or diploid. Any diploid cell may form an ascus when conditions are suitable. The nucleus divides by meiosis and 4 haploid ascospores are formed internally. When shed by rupture of the ascus or breakdown of its wall these grow vegetatively by budding, remaining as small haploid cells. In sexual reproduction these small haploid cells fuse in pairs to form larger diploid cells which continue to multiply

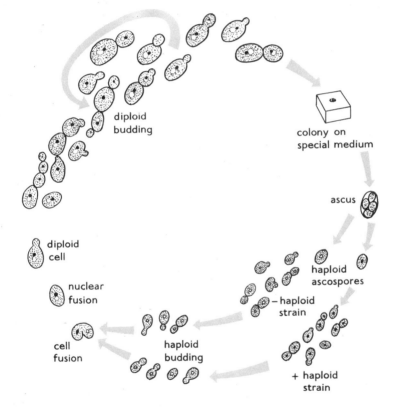

Fig. 8.1   Diagram of life cycle of *Saccharomyces cerevisiae*.

vigorously by budding as long as conditions are suitable for vegetative growth. When conditions change some of them may again form asci (Fig. 8.1). In other yeast species the diploid stage is represented only by the zygote which immediately forms an ascus and ascospores, only the haploid cells having the capacity for vegetative growth. In still other species only diploid cells grow by budding, the haploid ascospores germinating to form cells which immediately fuse in pairs.

TAPHRINALES

The species of the genus *Taphrina* are common plant parasites which resemble the yeasts in some respects. *T. deformans* causing peach leaf curl (Fig. 8.2) is well known and *T. coerulescens* causes similar puckering of oak

Fig. 8.2   Peach leaf curl caused by *Taphrina deformans*.

leaves. These fungi form a limited extent of mycelium in the intercellular spaces of leaves, the short hyphae consisting of binucleate cells. A mass of binucleate cells which form under the cuticle become asci. In each ascus the dikaryon fuses to become a diploid nucleus which immediately undergoes meiosis and 8 ascospores are formed. When these are shed (or even before this) they begin to grow by budding, forming numerous **blastospores** (the name given to spores produced by budding), some of which eventually grow into hyphae and infect new leaves. Within the young hypha the first nuclei pair to form a dikaryon and continue to divide simultaneously.

PLECTASCALES

The Eurotiaceae is a family of the order Plectascales, the commonly occurring and widespread species of which produce abundant mycelial growths which bear conidia prolifically. When asci are formed, they develop not singly as in the preceding examples, but in a larger or smaller group within a rounded fruiting body called the *ascocarp*. Where sexual reproduction has been observed in species of *Eurotium* antheridia and ascogonia (female gametangia) are formed from short hyphal branches which become coiled round one another. Antheridial contents apparently pass into the ascogonium where nuclei become paired. The ascogonium forms a cluster of small branches called *ascogenous hyphae*, all containing paired nuclei.

Asci in general are formed from ascogenous hyphae in a special way. A hyphal tip with a pair of nuclei bends sharply over to form a crook. The paired nuclei divide simultaneously, one daughter nucleus of each pair migrating into the elbow or top of the crook which is cut off by two cross-walls, one separating the tip containing one nucleus, and one cutting off the basal cell which also contains one nucleus. The elbow cell enlarges to form an ascus in which the paired nuclei fuse, then meiosis takes place and 4–8 haploid ascospores develop (Fig. 8.3). The surrounding hyphae grow together round the developing asci to form the ascocarp wall. As this fructification in *Eurotium* has no opening it is called a *cleistothecium*. At maturity it contains a mass of ascospores, the walls of the asci having disappeared.

Asexual reproduction

Almost as soon as species of *Eurotium* start to make a mycelial growth they begin to form conidia. Some of the multinucleate cells of the slender branching hyphae grow up into single-celled conidiophores, each with a swollen head covered with phialides. From the tips of these a succession of conidia are cut off in long chains. All known species of *Eurotium* bear this pattern of conidiophore which is the *Aspergillus* type (Fig. 8.4a). Many fungi have this type of conidiophore but they are not known to form asci. They are classified as species of *Aspergillus* which is one of the form-genera (genera described by asexual characters only) of the Fungi Imperfecti, the group in which are classified all fungi with no recognized sexual stages; *A. niger* is a common and important species.

The form-genus *Penicillium* of which a large number of species are recognized is closely similar to *Aspergillus*. The conidiophore is multicellular and is branched at the top to form a brush-like structure on which the tips of all the branches carry chains of conidia (Fig. 8.4b). Many form blue- or green-coloured colonies and grow commonly as moulds. The genus has become specially important since the discovery of penicillin.

Cleistothecia have been discovered in a few species of *Penicillium* showing that they also are Ascomycetes.

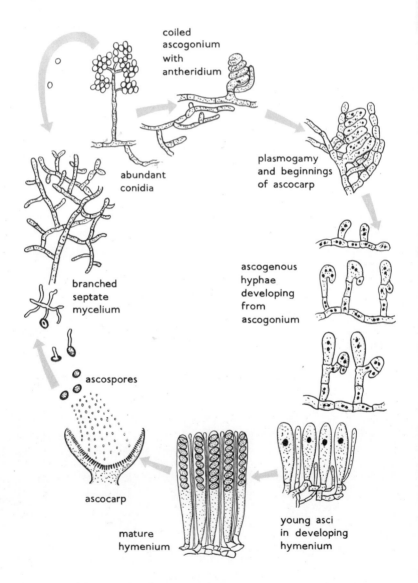

Fig. 8.3 Diagram of life cycle of hypothetical Ascomycete.

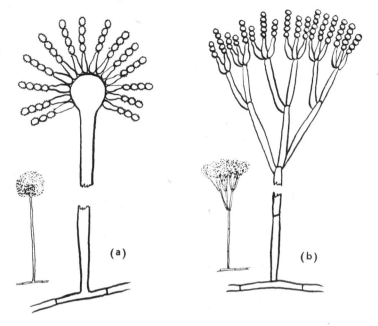

Fig. 8.4 Conidiophores of (a) *Aspergillus glaucus* (× c. 500) ; (b) *Penicillium notatum* (× c. 500).

Erysiphaceae

Another important family of the Plectascales is the Erysiphaceae which includes the powdery mildews, all of which are obligate parasites that cannot be cultured. The mycelium grows superficially on leaf surfaces pushing haustoria into epidermal cells. As soon as hyphae are established on leaf surfaces they form erect conidiophores from which successive conidia are cut off forming a dusty powder. These may infect other leaves.

Sexual reproduction

Details have been followed for some members of the group and it has been seen that small, uninucleate gametangia are formed on adjacent hyphae. After fusion and fertilization a cleistothecium develops in much the same way as in *Eurotium* and these structures may be seen on the leaf surfaces late in the season. Each of these small bodies may carry a number of radiating hyphal appendages which may be hair-like, hooked or branched and the whole structure is coloured orange to black.

SPHAERIALES

In the Sphaeriales asci are borne in flask-shaped structures called **perithecia**, each of which has a neck opening at the tip by an **ostiole**. On the interior perithecial surface the asci form a continuous layer called the **hymenium**. In the family Xylariaceae of this order ascocarps are typically dark brown or black and form hard, woody fruiting bodies. *Daldinia concentrica*, which grows commonly on dead or dying ash and other hardwoods, forms stromata like hemispheres of charcoal in which large numbers of perithecia are formed (Fig. 8.5). The black ascospores are shot out of the ascus which first elongates till the tip reaches the neck of the perithecium when it opens explosively. Empty asci shrink back into the fruiting body

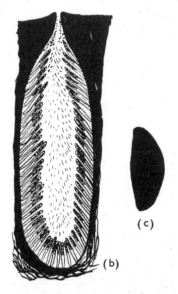

Fig. 8.5 *Daldinia concentrica*, the charcoal fungus : (a) fructification sectioned ($\times\frac{1}{2}$) ; (b) perithecium ($\times 66$) ; (c) spore ($\times 1,400$).

which discharges its spores over a period of months. In still air they make a sooty deposit on surrounding objects. Species of *Xylosphaera* are similar fungi which also grow on wood, forming black club-shaped stromata in which the perithecia are formed.

The Sphaeriales is a large order some species of which form brightly coloured stromata. A commonly occurring example is the parasite *Dialonectria galligena*, the cause of apple and pear canker disease. The fungus gains entry to susceptible twigs through wounds. The mycelium attacks and destroys sapwood causing the bark to collapse and crack into a canker. The fungus then grows on the surface of the wood forming spots each of

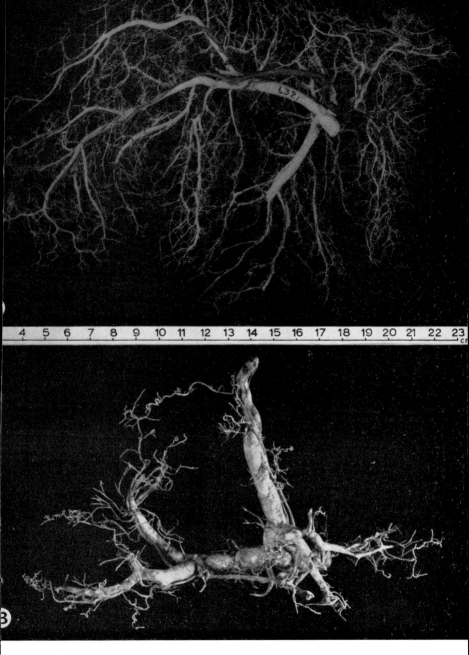

Plate 7 (A) Cast of bile ducts in a normal sheep's liver, together with some arteries (the darker vessels). (B) Cast of bile ducts in a sheep's liver damaged by the toxin from conidia of the fungus *Pithomyces chartarum* (p. 101); small vessels have disappeared, while the main ducts are grossly enlarged. (By courtesy of New Zealand Department of Agriculture.)

Plate 8 (**A**) Basal stem canker or black shank of tobacco caused by *Phytophthora parasitica* var. *nicotianae* (p. 130). (**B**) Deep culture tanks for large-scale production of vitamin B_{12}. (**C**) Plant for large-scale production of a new antibiotic. (A, courtesy of Cawthron Institute, Nelson, New Zealand; B and C, courtesy of Glaxo Laboratories Ltd., Greenford, Middlesex.)

which is a small, soft, pink stroma on which *Tubercularia*-type conidia are borne. This structure is called a ***sporodochium***. From its surface conidiophores arise producing large crescent-shaped, multiseptate conidia, each of which is capable of starting a new infection. Late in the season the stroma stops producing conidiophores and perithecia are formed within it. Ascogonia have been seen in the similar stromata of the common saprophyte *Nectria cinnabarina* (Fig. 8.6), and possibly spermatia which may fertilize

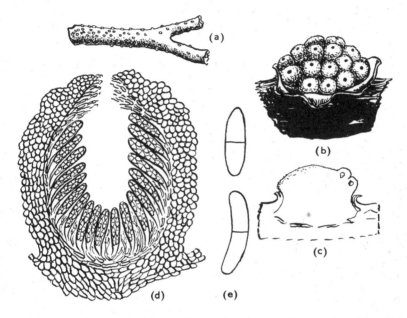

Fig. 8.6 *Nectria cinnabarina*, coral spot fungus: (a) fallen twig with pink stromata ($\times 1$) ; (b) cluster of perithecia ($\times 10$) ; (c) section of stroma largely in the conidial stage with 2 young perithecia ($\times 10$) ; (d) section of perithecium showing asci with biseriate septate spores ($\times 175$) ; (e) spores ($\times 1,000$). (In part after original drawings by Joan Dingley.)

them, but cytological details have not yet been worked out. Each perithecium formed by these fungi opens by a narrow neck through which the asci forcibly discharge their ascospores. Commonly the stromata with their perithecia survive the winter and in the following spring discharge ascospores which may start new infections.

Many imperfect fungi are known which produce only asexual spores of the same type as *D. galligena* and which are classified as species of *Tubercularia* in the Fungi Imperfecti. *Gibberella* (Fig. 8.7) is a genus placed close to *Nectria*.

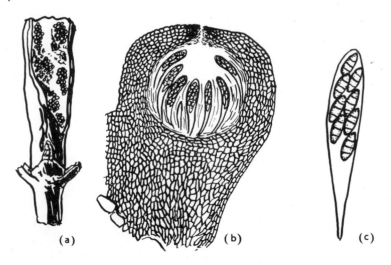

Fig. 8.7 *Gibberella macrolopha*: (a) canker with perithecia on *Coprosma robusta* stem (×3); (b) perithecium (×190); (c) ascus with biseriate septate spores (×560). (In part after original drawings by Joan Dingley.)

Claviceps

The fungus causing ergot, *Claviceps purpurea*, forms somewhat similar perithecia. The mycelium developing in infected ovaries of grasses in spring produces superficial hyphae and many conidiophores from which small rounded conidia are shed in a sticky, nectar-like secretion. Insects visit the flowers, feed on the nectar and distribute the conidia. By the time the grain is ripe infected ovaries have developed into elongated, dark purple sclerotia which drop to the ground where they remain dormant through the winter (Fig. 3.5). In spring they germinate forming tiny stalked stromata about 5 mm tall with rounded heads in which gametangia are formed. After the smaller antheridium has fused with the larger ascogonium a mass of dikaryotic ascogenous hyphae is formed at the base of each developing perithecium. The globose head of each stroma is dotted with the ostioles of many perithecia, each of which contains a number of elongated asci, in each of which lie 8 very long and very slender ascospores (Fig. 3.5). When mature these are discharged and may start a new infection. Selected strains of *Claviceps* are grown industrially for a supply of medicinal ergot alkaloids which are formed by the fungus in culture as well as in the naturally-produced sclerotia. The species of *Cordyceps* which mostly grow parasitically on insect larvae, mummifying them into vegetable caterpillar sclerotia, form similar stromata in which many perithecia are formed (Figs. 5.13, 5.14).

PEZIZALES

In another large group of Ascomycetes fruiting bodies are found in which the asci are developed in an extensive *hymenium* on a disc- or cup-shaped structure called an *apothecium.*

The Pezizales is a large order the many species of which form big or small disc- or cup-shaped apothecia on the surface of soil, rotting wood, etc. (Fig. 8.8). The hymenium lining the inside of the disc is often brightly

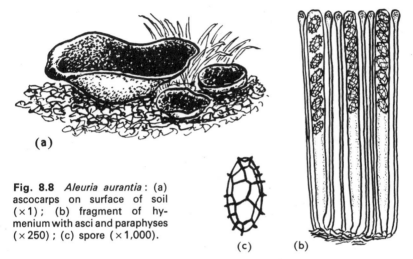

(a)

Fig. 8.8 *Aleuria aurantia* : (a) ascocarps on surface of soil (×1) ; (b) fragment of hymenium with asci and paraphyses (× 250) ; (c) spore (× 1,000).

(c)   **(b)**

coloured as in the common orange peel fungus, *Aleuria (Peziza) aurantia.* In this order the asci are operculate, each opening at the tip by a definite small, hinged lid. The ascospores are forcibly shot out and occasionally may be seen rising in a tiny cloud from one of these fructifications.

The genus *Morchella* includes the true morels, the apothecia of which are large stalked structures up to 6 in. tall bearing a large expanse of wrinkled, folded hymenium (Fig. 8.9a). These fructifications which appear in spring are highly prized as edible fungi. The mycelium is saprophytic, and presumably perennial, in soil. It grows readily on various sterile media but has never been induced to fruit in culture. *Helvella crispa*, which is seen fairly commonly in damp woods in autumn, is a somewhat similar large stalked Ascomycete (Fig. 8.9b).

An important related group includes the genera *Sclerotinia* and *Monilinia*, various species of which are important pathogens. *M. fructigena* is the well-known parasite causing brown rot of many kinds of stone fruit. Mycelium may invade blossom, young leaves or twigs but grows most

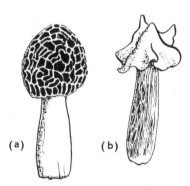

Fig. 8.9 Ascocarps of : (a) *Morchella esculenta* (×⅓) ; (b) *Helvella crispa* (×⅓).

readily in ripe fruit producing the characteristic brown rot. As soon as the mycelium is established it may start to form conidia on abundantly produced conidiophores which often arise in concentric rings round the starting-point of growth. The asexual form of the fungus has been classified in the genus *Monilia* of the Fungi Imperfecti and in this state it is still known as *M. fructigena* (Fig. 8.10). By its asexual spores the fungus may

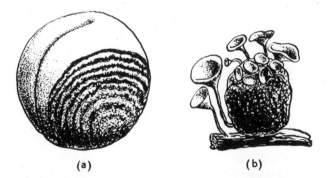

Fig. 8.10 *Monilinia fructigena* : (a) asexual growth forming banded colony on a rotting peach (×⅔) ; (b) apothecia growing from a mummified peach (×⅔).

spread widely. Entire fruits which first show characteristic brown spots are quickly invaded and the mycelium ramifies through the softened tissue which often shrivels and dries to a mummy full of a fungal stroma. This falls to the ground or may hang on the branches where it overwinters. In the spring the old stroma produces a fresh crop of conidia and so starts a new season's infections. It may rarely happen that shallow cup-shaped apothecia, each on a tiny stalk, grow out from the old stroma in spring;

ascogenous hyphae are formed within them and each becomes lined with hymenium from which ripe ascospores are shed to start new infections.

Many other fungi are known only in the *Monilia* form. The asexual state of described species of *Sclerotinia* is in the form of *Botrytis*, a familiar genus of Fungi Imperfecti some species of which are known only in the asexual stage. *B. cinerea*, grey mould, is a very common facultative parasite. In the genus *Sclerotinia* the stalked apothecia arise from a sclerotium.

TUBERALES

The Tuberales is a special group in which the fructifications are formed underground and are like small tubers. The hymenium is internal and is exposed only when the tuber is broken or decays. The asci are swollen structures which contain large or even enormous spores. In *Tuber macrosporum* spores reach $80 \times 45\ \mu$ (Fig. 8.11). The European truffle of commerce which is a specially good, edible fungus is *T. melanosporum*. It is

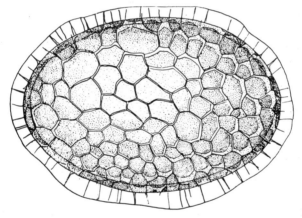

Fig. 8.11   *Tuber macrosporum* ascospore ($\times$1,000).

found usually under oak trees. The species of this group are probably mainly mycorrhizal fungi as their distribution seems to be linked to that of certain trees.

LABOULBENIALES

The Laboulbeniales is a numerous group of obligate parasites of insects. The thalli are very small structures growing on the exoskeletons of the

insects which do not seem to be much affected by them. They form small
male and female gametangia from which a single ascus develops. Asexual
spores are unknown. The group is rather distinct from other Ascomycetes.

LOCULOASCOMYCETES

A sub-class, the Loculoascomycetes, includes a considerable number of
saprophytes and parasites all of which have bitunicate asci, i.e. with a
double wall. Most of the fungi in this distinct group form small, dark perithecia in stromata which often occur as black spots on various parts of
higher plants. *Venturia inaequalis* which causes the all too common apple
scab is a troublesome parasite wherever apples are grown. *Botryosphaeria
dothidea* (Fig. 8.12a) makes black spots on stems of many woody plants

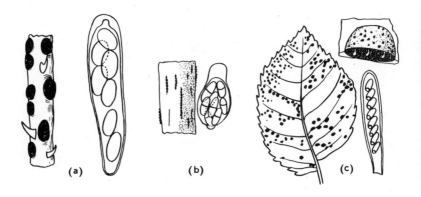

Fig. 8.12 Examples of Loculoascomycetidae: (a) *Botryosphaeria dothidea*;
(b) *Mycosphaerella lineolata*; (c) *Euryachora ulmi*. (Redrawn. Courtesy of the
Ray Society, London.)

including rose. Species of *Mycosphaerella* (Fig. 8.12b) appear as black
spots on many kinds of leaves and *M. fragariae* is often seen on strawberry
plants. *Euryachora ulmi* (Fig. 8.12c) forms black spots on fallen elm leaves
while dead birch leaves are commonly dotted with similar stromata of
E. betulina. Rhopographus filicinus frequently grows on old bracken stems
making small, elongated black pustules which are seen only on close
examination. In each of these tiny fructifications there is a group of more
or less closed perithecia containing the characteristic asci.

TRENDS IN THE ASCOMYCETES

The rather narrow, more or less regularly septate hyphae of Asco-mycetes, often forming fungal 'tissues', are quite unlike those of the classes treated in the previous chapter. The Ascomycetes are typically fungi of drier terrestrial habitats and do not form any motile cells, points of further contrast with the lower groups. The only true diploid phase is the briefly existing zygote or fusion nucleus of the ascus which immediately divides by meiosis. The formation of paired nuclei in the ascogenous hyphae which follow fertilization of gametangia or fusion of vegetative hyphae is an important distinctive character. The proliferation of these dikaryotic cells precedes the formation of large numbers of sexual spores together in different forms of ascocarp (cleistothecia, perithecia and apothecia), and the development of these in macroscopic fruiting bodies results in the sexual spores being generally more important for the spread of the fungus than they are in the earlier classes. In spite of the efficiency of much asco-spore production it is the asexual spores of Ascomycetes which are their most striking feature as they are produced in exceptional abundance almost continuously during mycelial growth. For a very large number of species this asexual reproduction appears to have been sufficient for survival for so long that these fungi have lost the ability to produce sexual spores and thus have become stabilized as forms which we classify in the Fungi Imperfecti. Most of these can be identified with the asexual stages of known Asco-mycetes though a few may be degenerate Basidiomycetes. Some which grow only as sterile mycelium are unidentifiable.

For some Ascomycetes sex organs are regularly formed and fusion of gametangia, which are often coiled, precedes the development of dikaryons and, later, asci. In many species sex organs have not been seen, the asco-genous hyphae apparently arising from fusion of vegetative hyphae. In a few species the ascogonium has a long slender process called a trichogyne to which male cells become attached before fusion, a condition which has suggested relationship to red algae. In other respects, however, Asco-mycetes seem far removed from algae so that the similarity is thought to be the result of parallel evolution rather than of direct relationship.

9

Basidiomycetes

This is the most advanced group of fungi, distinguished from the others characteristically by the production of the sexual spores, basidiospores, as external buds on the basidium. Although the present accepted number of species for the class is exceeded by the total of Ascomycetes, it is thought that the Basidiomycetes is probably the largest group of fungi because many more species await discovery and description (Fig. 5.1). The large fruiting bodies formed by the higher orders are a conspicuous feature of the vegetation of most parts of the world but, because of their seasonal occurrence and of the difficulty of their correct identification, the distribution of the many kinds is still imperfectly known. The main orders of the group are as follows:

Ustilaginales (smut fungi).
Uredinales (rust fungi).
Tremellales (gelatinous fungi).
Aphyllophorales (including brackets and fairy clubs).
Agaricales (toadstools).
Gasteromycetales (puff-balls and others).

Examples to illustrate the important features of each of these orders are given below.

USTILAGINALES

The smut fungi which are specialized plant parasites capable of making limited, often yeast-like, growth in culture, are of world-wide occurrence and may be found on many kinds of plants. Those which attack grain are of considerable economic importance though they are less common than formerly because the almost universal use of chemical seed dressings kills the majority of the fungal spores which the seed may carry. There are many variations in details of the life history of different smut fungi of which the following is one example.

Ustilago avenae causes loose smut of oats, a widely distributed disease. All the grains in an affected head become replaced by a sooty mass of black smut spores which may blow about at maturity and lodge in healthy heads. Diseased spikelets which go through the threshing machine will provide spores to contaminate the bulk of the grain. When any such grain is used for seed it carries the smut or brand spores with it. Each smut spore (or teliospore) is binucleate and when this germinates on or close to the sprouting seed the two nuclei fuse and immediately afterwards the fusion nucleus undergoes meiosis. A slender hypha grows out to form a promycelium or basidium which contains the haploid nuclei. Slender basidiospores, each containing a haploid nucleus, are budded from the promycelium. Repeated budding may result in the formation of a large number of these small basidiospores which are also called sporidia. Fusion takes place between pairs of sporidia to form a dikaryotic hypha capable of infecting the coleoptile of the seedling. This dikaryotic mycelium grows very sparsely within the seedling without damaging it, but remaining as occasional clusters of intercellular hyphae below the growing point. At flowering time the fungus may extend to the spikelets and grow abundantly within the developing ovaries finally replacing the grain with a smutty mass of the binucleate teliospores or brand spores (Plate 3C and D).

UREDINALES

The rust fungi are extremely numerous and also of great importance. They are obligate parasites attacking all sorts of higher plants causing damage and loss in various crops. Rusts are characterized by up to five different spore forms in the life cycle which may be developed on two successive hosts, a phenomenon called **heteroecism**. Spores formed on the first host infect the second, and vice versa. Rusts which develop all stages on one host are **autoecious**. Those which develop all possible spore forms are **long cycle** rusts, while those which omit one or more are called **short cycle** rusts. Some species are heterothallic, others homothallic.

Puccinia graminis, which causes the serious disease of black stem rust of wheat and which may also attack other susceptible grasses and grains, is an example of a heteroecious, long cycle rust, the life cycle of which is shown diagrammatically in Fig. 9.1. The dark, thick-walled, two-celled, dikaryotic **teliospores** (teleutospores) are formed in black **telia** (teleutosori) which appear on infected grasses late in summer. These spores overwinter on the soil and germinate in the following spring. In each cell the dikaryon

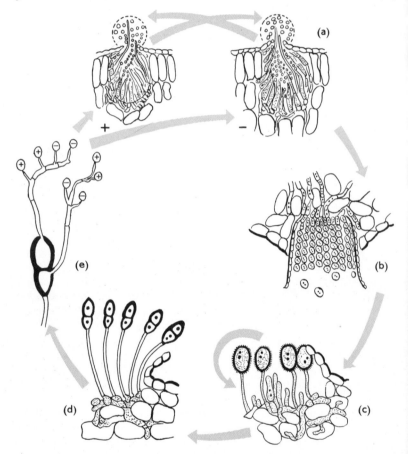

Fig. 9.1. Diagram of life cycle of *Puccinia graminis.*   (See cycle opposite.)

fuses to form a zygote nucleus which immediately undergoes meiosis. The cell contents grow out and form a slender, 4-celled promycelium with one nucleus in each cell. A sterigma is formed on each division and a small haploid **basidiospore** is budded off, then forcibly discharged from the basidial sterigma and blown away on the wind. Each is capable of continued growth only if it reaches a barberry bush.

When a basidiospore germinates on a barberry leaf it produces a limited infection due to growth of haploid mycelium. *P. graminis* is heterothallic and each haploid mycelium is of either a plus or a minus strain. On the upper surface of the leaves the haploid infection forms small flask-shaped structures called **pycnia** (spermogonia) from which masses of small

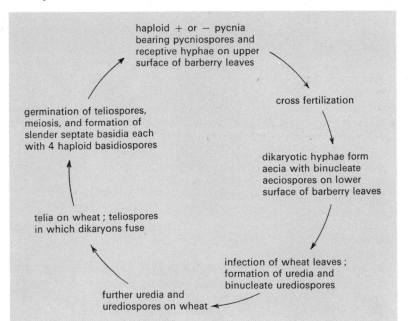

haploid + or − pycnia
bearing pycniospores and
receptive hyphae on upper
surface of barberry leaves

cross fertilization

germination of teliospores,
meiosis, and formation of
slender septate basidia each
with 4 haploid basidiospores

dikaryotic hyphae form
aecia with binucleate
aeciospores on lower
surface of barberry leaves

telia on wheat ; teliospores
in which dikaryons fuse

infection of wheat leaves ;
formation of uredia and
binucleate urediospores

further uredia and
urediospores on wheat

uninucleate cells called **pycniospores** (spermatia) are exuded in droplets of
nectar. There are also receptive hyphae in the necks of the pycnia. Insects
collecting the nectar distribute the pycniospores, and when these are
transferred to receptive hyphae of the opposite strain fusion follows and
dikaryotic hyphae are formed.

The dikaryotic mycelium grows through the barberry leaves and produces tiny cup-shaped sori, **aecia** (aecidia), on the under surface. In each
of these, chains of binucleate **aeciospores** are formed and are blown away
by the wind (Fig. 9.1).They cannot reinfect barberry but if they reach a
susceptible grass host they establish a new infection of binucleate mycelium.
Each infection is of limited extent with a small growth of intercellular
hyphae which push haustoria into some of the living cells. Very soon
clusters of cells form a **uredium** (uredosorus) with **urediospores** under
the grass epidermis which then bursts open exposing a mass of the rust-
coloured spores. These have moderately thick spiny walls and are produced
in great abundance. As they readily infect more grain plants and produce
similar lesions, an infected field may soon be producing clouds of these
rusty urediospores. As the season progresses the rusty pustules begin to
produce some dark, 2-celled teliospores till finally the uredia develop into
black telia producing only the thick-walled, two-celled spores.

Many strains of *P. graminis* are known as this species has developed a high degree of *biological specialization*, many individual races being restricted each to one particular variety of cultivated grain. Control of the disease on wheat depends on breeding rust-resistant varieties, but continual watch is necessary for new strains of the fungus with a different host range. Eradication of barberry in wheat-growing districts both in Europe and America, where it was formerly widely used as a hedge plant, has not greatly reduced the incidence of wheat rust because air-borne urediospores may travel long distances (p. 76), but it helps to prevent new strains arising by hybridization. However, fusions are also known to occur among dikaryotic mycelia of different origins with exchange of nuclei and thus of genetic material, so that in effect hybridization is possible, even if infrequent, in the absence of a normal sexual stage.

Another example of a long cycle heteroecious rust is *Cronartium ribicola* which produces pycnia and aecia on *Pinus strobus* and other five-needle pines, the foliage of which is often seriously damaged, while the uredia and telia occur on species of *Ribes* (p. 96). In this case eradication of *Ribes* effectively controls the disease on *Pinus*.

Puccinia malvacearum, the hollyhock rust, is an example of a short cycle autoecious homothallic rust which forms only telia and teliospores on the single host. These germinate in the same way as those of *P. graminis*, producing a promycelium and haploid basidiospores which reinfect hollyhock leaves. Dikaryotic mycelium develops after vegetative fusions and then teliospores are again formed.

TREMELLALES

This order is a large group the species of which produce definite fruiting bodies, or *sporophores*, often large structures, more or less gelatinous in texture. They may stand drying and rewetting. The basidia, which are formed in an extensive layer of closely-packed cells called the *hymenium*, are usually septate thus resembling the promycelia formed by smut and rust fungi, and in some the basidiospores may further reproduce by budding. The simple yeast-like fungi of the Sporobolomycetaceae, the spores of which are so commonly air-borne, are thought by some to be related to this group.

APHYLLOPHORALES

A diverse assortment of families is gathered in this large order. Most of the species produce large fructifications, in the Polyporaceae in the form of brackets, in the Clavariaceae as clubs or in other families as different forms. A number are important tree parasites, many also attack timber. The fructifications of this group may be made from woven hyphae of a single type, or from two or three distinct kinds of hyphae, and then are described as **monomitic, dimitic** or **trimitic**. Hyphal cells of special forms and shapes may occur both in the body of the sporophore and also in the hymenium (Fig. 9.2). These anatomical details are constant for each species

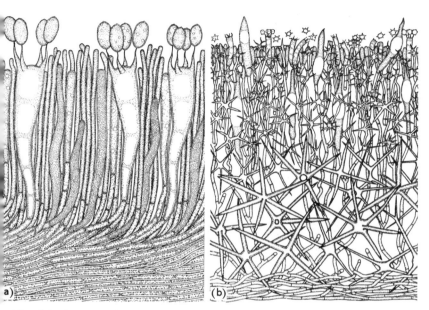

Fig. 9.2 Sections of hymenium of species of Aphyllophorales : (a) *Aleurodiscus ochraceo-flavus* (×275) ; (b) *Asterostroma persimile* (×250). (After Cunningham, G. H., 1956, *Trans. R. Soc. N.Z.*, **84**, 248 ; **83**, 244.)

and hence are useful and important in classification. The mycelium of these fungi is often long-lived, even perennial, and grows in soil, litter, fallen wood, etc., which it permeates. When favourable conditions follow after enough food material has been accumulated the mycelium forms its conspicuous fruiting body with the hymenium exposed on some part of its surface. The following are examples of genera and species of this order.

Sparassis crispa (Fig. 9.3d) with edible cauliflower-like fructifications grows typically at the base of pine trees. *Hydnum repandum* (Fig. 9.3a) which bears its hymenium over the surface of teeth is another edible species. The pale flesh-coloured sporophores are found commonly in autumn in mixed woods. *Cantharellus cibarius* (Fig. 9.3b) is the apricot-coloured chanterelle, a familiar sight in autumn in the markets of European towns where it is prized for cooking. It grows under most of our woodland trees. *Craterellus cornucopioides* (Fig. 9.3c), another good edible species, occurs fairly commonly under beech and oak trees.

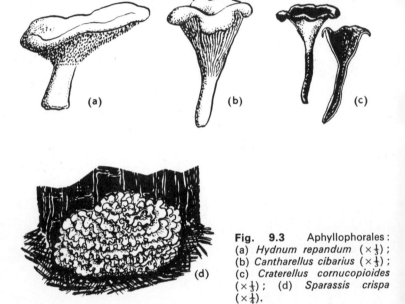

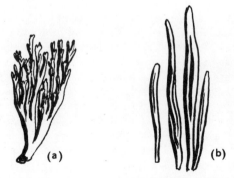

Fig. 9.3 Aphyllophorales: (a) *Hydnum repandum* ($\times\frac{1}{3}$); (b) *Cantharellus cibarius* ($\times\frac{1}{3}$); (c) *Craterellus cornucopioides* ($\times\frac{1}{3}$); (d) *Sparassis crispa* ($\times\frac{1}{4}$).

Many species of the genus *Clavaria* and its close relatives grow in soil and rotting timber. The club-shaped or coral-like fructifications, called fairy fingers, are brightly coloured and are often conspicuous in autumn (Fig. 9.4a,b).

Fig. 9.4 Aphyllophorales: (a) *Clavaria cinerea* ($\times\frac{2}{3}$); (b) *C. fusiformis* ($\times\frac{2}{3}$).

Serpula (syn. *Merulius*) *lacrymans*, the dry rot fungus, is a notorious member of this order. The fructification is **resupinate** appearing as a bright yellow, fleshy crust on the outside of rotting timber. The surface of the crust is wrinkled or may have a mass of shallow pores, and is covered with hymenium. As the mycelium actively digests cellulose but not lignin, it reduces timber to a soft brown mass and so is said to cause a brown rot. The wood cracks regularly into cubical structures thus forming a characteristic brown cubical rot. Cellulose is often hydrolysed so rapidly that drops of water collect on the fungus, hence its epithet. It often establishes itself in damp buildings where serious damage may ensue. Rhizomorphs are usually formed and may travel long distances over indigestible material, such as brickwork, and establish new infections. Care in keeping buildings

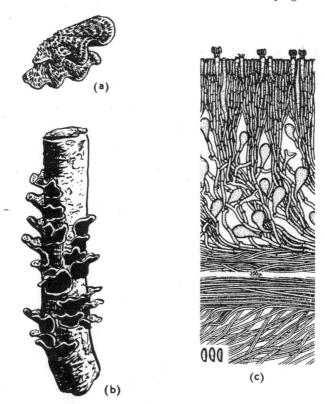

Fig. 9.5 Aphyllophorales: (a) *Stereum hirsutum* ($\times \frac{2}{3}$); (b) *S, purpureum* fructifications on plum ($\times \frac{2}{3}$); (c) section of same ($\times 250$), spores ($\times 500$) (after Cunningham, G. H., 1956, *Trans. R. Soc. N.Z.*, **84**, 227).

dry and well ventilated is the most important protective measure against dry rot, but chemical treatments are used to halt old infections, or to prevent new outbreaks of disease where conditions make them possible.

Stereum purpureum (Fig. 9.5b, c) is a serious parasite which attacks and often kills many kinds of fruit and ornamental trees, especially of the family Rosaceae. It also grows vigorously as a saprophyte on old stumps and felled wood. The first outward symptom on a diseased tree is a silvering of the foliage, so the disease is called silver leaf. After the mycelium has made extensive growth within the host sporophores are formed on the dead or dying branches. They appear as thin, papery brackets with a greyish, tomentose upper surface and a smooth, purplish hymenium covering the lower surface. *S. purpureum* is a species capable of digesting both lignin and cellulose and so causes a white rot, reducing the diseased wood to a friable white mass. A very common saprophytic species found often on fallen wood is *S. hirsutum* (Fig. 9.5a).

Species of the genus *Polyporus*, and of some closely related to it, include many tree pathogens and timber-rotting fungi. The fructifications generally are well-developed, corky or woody brackets with a layer of pores containing the hymenium covering the under surface. The following are important examples of this group of genera.

Phaeolus (syn. *Polyporus*) *schweinitzii*, which forms hard irregular brackets of a rusty brown colour with a furry upper surface and large irregular pores, causes a brown cubical rot of pine heart wood, and fairly commonly attacks pines in Europe causing butt rot. It digests cellulose only and the softened brown residue cracks regularly into cubes. The fungus may gain entry to the base of the tree through roots or through a wound.

Fomes annosus represents a genus which forms large, perennial woody brackets on which a fresh layer of pores with hymenium is formed annually. The upper surface of the bracket has an irregular, bubbly crust of a reddish-brown while the pore surface is white (Fig. 9.6a). *F. annosus* causes a butt rot or a serious heart rot of conifers in which the rotted wood is left in a characteristic form with small white pockets, a so-called white pocket rot. It also attacks broad-leaved trees and structural timbers. *F. pinicola* is a species less important in Europe than in America where it is a cause of serious heart rot of coniferous trees.

Ganoderma applanatum is a serious parasite of dicotyledonous trees, especially old beeches, in which it causes damaging heart rot in the form of a white mottled rot. The fructifications form large, perennial, woody, shelf-like brackets, brown above, paler below at first but soon becoming brown. Clouds of brown spores from the large brackets may coat surrounding bark and foliage (Fig. 9.6b).

Trametes gibbosa, which forms very regular, small, flat brackets, whitish in colour, is a common saprophyte on stumps of beech, oak and other broad-leaved trees. The upper surface is densely tomentose while the lower surface has large irregular pores. The texture of the whole fungus is tough and corky (Fig. 9.6c).

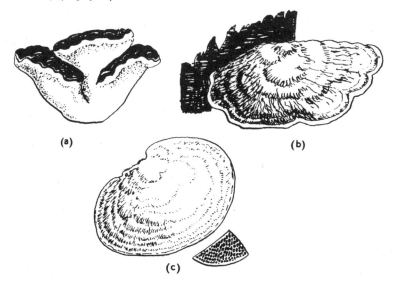

Fig. 9.6 Aphyllophorales : (a) *Fomes annosus* ($\times\frac{1}{3}$) ; (b) *Ganoderma applanatum* ($\times\frac{1}{6}$) ; (c) *Trametes gibbosa* ($\times\frac{2}{3}$).

AGARICALES

The fungi of this order produce fleshy sporophores in the form of the well-known toadstools, of which many thousands of species have been described, yet new ones are continually being discovered. Popular interest in them arises mainly from the desirability of many for food, though the dangerously poisonous nature of others has to be considered also. For many amateurs they are things of beauty and a source of great interest. Some species fruit regularly in the same place each year, others are seen only at long intervals. The production of sporophores appears to be favoured by a spell of mild, wet weather following a dry period, so that in temperate regions toadstools appear in abundance in the autumn. The hymenium is spread over the gills which hang in radial arrangement beneath the cap. These lamellae may be exposed from an early stage of development, but in many species they are enclosed till nearly mature and then become exposed to the air. In some genera the gills fork repeatedly, while in the *Boletus* group they are replaced by soft pores. Anatomical characters are often useful in classifying agarics, the fructifications of which frequently have modified hyphae and hyphal cells, though they do not show the regular development of the different hyphal systems that are often found in members of the Aphyllophorales. Special cells known as **cystidia** (Fig. 9.10) are often present on gill margins or faces. An indication of the chemical nature of hyphal walls, a feature which is of importance in classification, can be obtained often by staining, iodine being widely used for this purpose. The colour of the spore deposit is characteristic of different genera and may be seen when the spores are collected as a print.

The development of *Amanita rubescens*, the blusher, illustrates the main macroscopic features of toadstools. The mycelium which grows commonly in the soil of woods in the north temperate zone usually forms fructifications abundantly in autumn. These appear first as egg-like structures at the soil surface, completely enclosed in an outer membrane called the **universal veil**. As the toadstool grows this veil is broken and partly disintegrates. Part of it remains round the base of the **stem** or **stipe** where it forms a **volva**, and part remains as flecks or scales on top of the cap or **pileus**. As the stipe lengthens and the pileus expands another membrane called the **partial veil** is seen to cover the **gills** or **lamellae**. When the pileus extends this, also, is broken and part remains as a **ring**, or **annulus**, on the stem (Fig. 9.7). Occasionally part of the partial veil persists as a fringe

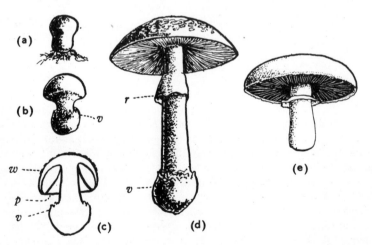

Fig. 9.7 Agaricales : (a–d) *Amanita rubescens* ($\times \frac{1}{3}$) : (a) early stage of sporo-phore enclosed in universal veil ; (b) later stage with universal veil broken to form a volva, *v*, at base of stipe, gills still enclosed by partial veil ; (c) section of similar stage : *w*, warts from universal veil, *p*, partial veil ; (d) sporophore with expanded pileus : *r*, ring or annulus formed from partial veil ; (e) *Agaricus campestris* sporophore ($\times \frac{1}{3}$).

bordering the pileus. When the gills are freely exposed the pileus is usually orientated so that they hang exactly vertically. As the gills mature the spores are shot off singly into the spaces between the gills and fall into the air currents flowing below the pileus. In this genus they are colourless, appearing white in a mass. Although *A. rubescens*, a very common species, is edible, this genus includes the most deadly poisonous of all known toadstools, *A. phalloides* and *A. verna*, and other poisonous species as well. *Amanita* species have both a universal and a partial veil but in most other genera one or both are missing.

Agaricus species include the best-known edible fungi used in British countries, though other European peoples are much more adventurous in this matter and use many other kinds for cooking also (Fig. 9.7e). In *Agaricus* species there is no universal veil and the young mushroom appears initially as a button with a shank, the stipe. The gills are at first enclosed by a partial veil which ruptures to form a conspicuous ring on the stem. The hymenium covering the gills appears pink at first, but soon darkens to a deep purplish-brown as the spores mature. When shed the spores have dark walls and form a purplish-black print.

Many fungi produce volatile compounds with a smell characteristic of the species, and as the nose is a sensitive organ capable of detecting a very low concentration of such substances it is usual for mycologists to sniff at their specimens. Edible mushrooms have a readily recognized, characteristic smell. The wild *Agaricus* species, several of which are good to eat, have four-spored basidia but the cultivated varieties all produce two-spored basidia.

Coprinus comatus, the shaggy cap or large ink cap, is a very good edible toadstool (Fig. 9.8a). All *Coprinus* species show a curious feature in the maturing gills which are white at first, then pink, but gradually blacken from the margin of the pileus back toward the stipe as the dark-walled spores mature. The gills are very thin and crowded, but once their maturity is reached and their spores shed they quickly pass into a senescent stage when they liquefy in a process of autodigestion and their substance disappears in inky droplets. Old ink cap toadstools may be seen with only the stipe standing crowned by a smudge of ink.

Armillaria mellea, the honey agaric, is the dreaded boot-lace parasite which may kill many different kinds of trees, usually by attacking the roots, but also causing a white rot of the heart wood. It grows abundantly also as a saprophyte. As a parasite it occurs mainly on trees weakened or damaged in some way. The typical black rhizomorphs may spread the infection from diseased stumps to new trees and often may be found running under the bark and then out into surrounding soil (Fig. 3.2a). The honey-coloured toadstools fruit in bunches on old infected stems which may become covered with a white spore deposit. When growing vigorously the mycelium

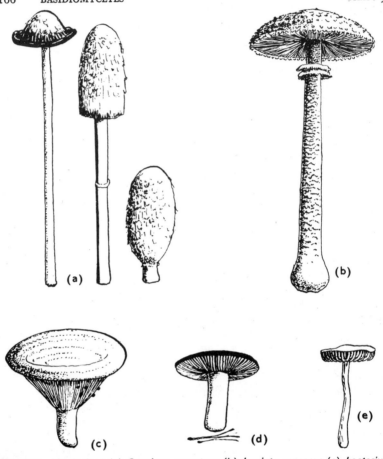

Fig. 9.8 Agaricales : (a) *Coprinus comatus* ; (b) *Lepiota procera* ; (c) *Lactarius deliciosus* with drops of milk ; (d) *Russula emetica* ; (e) *Laccaria laccata* (all × ⅓).

is *luminescent* so that rotting wood infected by this fungus glows in the dark. A number of other unrelated agarics are also luminescent. Some found in New Guinea and New Caledonia give enough light from one pileus for a man camping in the bush to read by.

Species of *Lepiota* (Fig. 9.8b) are white-spored agarics which have a very well developed ring on the stalk but no volva.

Lactarius and *Russula* (Fig. 9.8c, d) are two related genera represented by numerous brightly coloured species. Both have sculptured amyloid spores (staining blue or grey with iodine) and characteristically brittle flesh which in *Lactarius* species produces milk from lactiferous vessels extending through the sporophore. In autumn many kinds are found commonly in woods where they may be mycorrhizal or litter-destroying fungi.

Species of *Marasmius* and *Collybia*, which are rather tough toadstools, are often found attached to litter and appear to be important in primary stages of its decomposition. *Marasmius* species will revive after drying if they are moistened. *Laccaria laccata* (Fig. 9.8e), probably the commonest toadstool in the world, is a small brick-coloured species with spiny spores.

Cortinarius is a toadstool genus characterized by brown spores and by a partial veil in the form of a delicate web or cortina which collapses on to the stipe leaving only a trace of a ring. Many are brightly coloured and also often glutinous. Individual species may be characteristically associated with certain species of trees with which they form mycorrhizas.

The species of *Boletus* and related genera are large fleshy toadstools which have the hymenium developed in a layer of fleshy pores instead of gills (Fig. 9.9a). They are not closely related to the woody bracket fungi which also have pores, but rather to the toadstool genus *Paxillus* which has thick, frequently forking gills (Fig. 9.9b). Many species of these genera are mycorrhizal and are important for the growth of the trees with which they are associated.

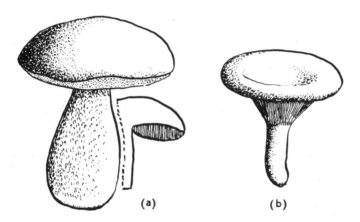

Fig. 9.9 Agaricales : (a) *Boletus edulis* ($\times \frac{1}{3}$) ; (b) *Paxillus involutus* ($\times \frac{1}{3}$).

The **mycelium** which forms the toadstool is dikaryotic though in a few agaric species parts of the fruiting body, such as some of the veil cells, may revert to the monokaryotic condition and have been used to start mono-karyotic cultures. For a majority of the species the dikaryotic mycelium shows frequent clamp connections (Fig. 1.5) which are regularly formed in narrow hyphae, though they may be missing from parts of the fruiting body built of wide hyphae. The presence of clamps is a useful diagnostic character for those species and genera which have them. The gill tissue or **trama** is made up of hyphae arranged systematically, in some species more or less parallel, in others more or less divergent, or ending centrally (inverse), or hyphae may be irregularly woven (Fig. 9.10).

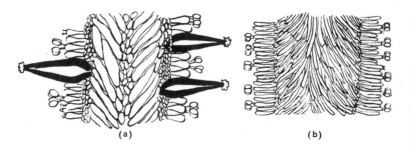

Fig. 9.10 Agaricales; t.s. of gills: (a) inverse trama, special thick-walled cystidia (metuloids) on gill faces; (b) bilateral trama.

The **basidium** is a somewhat swollen, terminal dikaryotic cell in which nuclear fusion takes place, followed immediately by a meiosis (Fig. 1.5b). Four slender pointed outgrowths, the sterigmata, at the tip of the basidium, each form a spore by a budding process and one haploid nucleus migrates through the narrow sterigma into each. A tiny droplet of water forms at one side of the junction and then each basidiospore in turn is shot off with its adhering droplet for a distance of o·1–1 mm, after which it falls between the gills. This mechanism, which can be observed in many Basidiomycetes, appears to operate by a spore of higher turgor pressure suddenly splitting free from a low-pressure basidium.

Each basidiospore is a potential starting-point for a haploid monokaryotic mycelium. Many agarics have been proved in culture to be heterothallic, as probably most are. When two monokaryotic mycelia of opposite strain meet fusion of hyphae occurs, nuclei migrate and dikaryons are formed (Fig. 9.11). Under ordinary conditions most agaric mycelium is dikaryotic as numerous spores may germinate together. Basidiospores are produced in such profusion, thousands of millions from each large toadstool, that it is obvious that these are the important spore forms in the Agaricales, only a few members of which produce asexual spores.

The mycelia of most agarics can be cultured, but only a few, mainly coprophilous species, fruit in culture. Specifically identified cultures may be started from spores or from fragments of sporophores, but when isolations of agaric-type mycelia are made from soil there is no way of knowing to what species they belong. Under ordinary culture conditions other kinds of soil fungi grow much more readily and the agarics are not recovered in soil isolations. The many thousands of species of agarics which grow in soil are known by their toadstools, but apart from mycorrhizal partners very little is understood about what the agaric mycelium does in its normal environment.

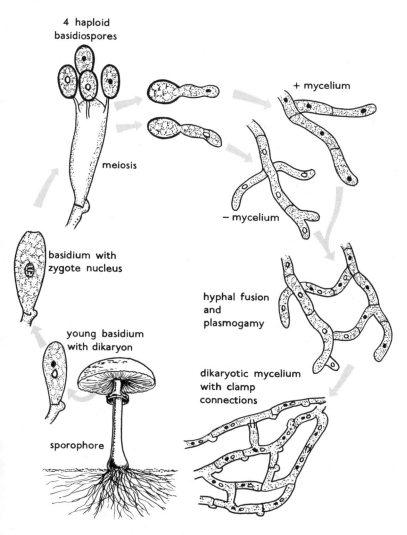

Fig. 9.11 Diagram of life cycle of hypothetical agaric.

GASTEROMYCETALES

In this group which includes about 1,000 species the sporophore is an enclosed structure with an outer covering called a **peridium**. The hymenium lines folds of internal tissue forming a central sporogenous mass called the **gleba**. Basidiospores are shed into internal spaces at maturity and are then liberated, either through some opening developing in the enclosed structure, or simply by its rupture and decay. The form of the sporophore is varied and the order may be polyphyletic.

The genus *Lycoperdon* includes the common puff-balls which may appear like golf balls in the grass. Some species are covered with rough or pointed warts. At maturity a pore appears in the peridium opening to the dusty gleba. When the ripe sporophore is hit by rain drops or wind-driven debris puffs of spores are released (Fig. 9.12a).

Calvatia gigantea is the well-known giant puff-ball which often reaches 1 or 2 ft in diameter and occasionally is even larger. At maturity the peridium is thin and papery and breaks away exposing a colossal mass of gleba with millions of millions of spores.

Geastrum species are earth stars in which the peridium separates into

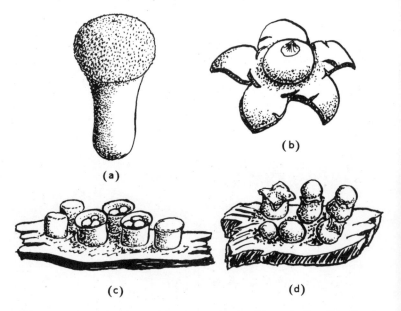

(a)

(b)

(c)

(d)

Fig. 9.12 Gasteromycetales: (a) *Lycoperdon perlatum* ($\times \frac{3}{4}$); (b) *Geastrum triplex* ($\times \frac{1}{2}$); (c) *Crucibulum vulgare* ($\times 1$); (d) *Sphaerobolus stellatus* ($\times 5$).

two or three distinct layers, the outermost of which splits and peels back to form rays. This may hold the small, ball-shaped inner peridium which opens at maturity by a central pore surrounded by slender teeth through which the dusty spores escape (Fig. 9.12b).

Crucibulum species, or bird's-nest fungi, are like tiny balls which open in the form of a small cup or nest. The gleba is divided into a number of small separate bodies called **peridiola** which form the eggs in the nest. In some species these are ejected by raindrops splashing into the cups and driving the peridiola several feet (Fig. 9.12c).

Sphaerobolus stellatus, a tiny species of special interest, is a related fungus occurring fairly commonly on fallen twigs and old sticks. It forms clusters of ball-like sporophores about 2 mm in diameter. These open in a star formation to make small cups in each of which lies a glebal ball about 1 mm across. The peridial wall of the tiny cups is two-layered, the outer layer fixed to the twigs with the inner layer hanging loosely inside it fixed only at the star points. At maturity the peridium acts as a catapult. Suddenly the inner wall is blown out and shoots the tiny, sticky glebal ball 4 or 5 m. It remains stuck to anything it may hit. This interesting mechanism is light sensitive, the peridial stars shooting their glebal balls towards the light (Fig. 9.12d).

Phallus is an example of the stinkhorns, the species of which produce partly gelatinous sporophores with foetid, sticky gleba. The common stinkhorn, *P. impudicus*, appears first as a soft egg with a thin leathery skin which bursts to expose the gelatinous contents. After the egg opens a crumpled white stalk rapidly elongates to a height of about 15 cm, carrying the evil-smelling gleba up into the air. Flies are soon attracted and distribute the spores (Fig. 9.13a). *Ileodictyon cibarius* (Fig. 9.13c) and *Aseroe rubra* (Fig. 9.13b) are common Australasian phalloids with similar gelatinous texture and dark, stinking gleba.

TRENDS IN THE BASIDIOMYCETES

These higher fungi are mostly very much smaller organisms than the higher plants but, nevertheless, like all fungi form a very important part of our environment. Those which are obviously of economic importance have been well studied, but little is known of the physiology and properties of many others.

The smuts and rusts arc highly-developed parasites, the life histories of which show many special features. The heteroecious rusts with a high degree of biological specialization are widespread plant parasites. They are the only Basidiomycetes which develop definite sex cells. For all others no sex organs or cells are involved in the formation of the dikaryotic mycelium.

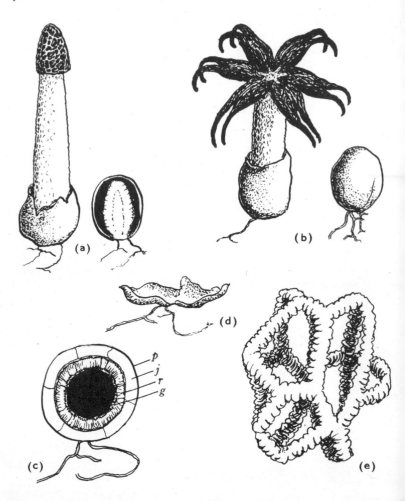

Fig. 9.13 Gasteromycetales: (a) *Phallus impudicus* expanded sporophore and section of unopened 'egg' ($\times \frac{1}{3}$); (b) *Aseroe rubra* sporophore and 'egg' ($\times \frac{2}{3}$); (c) *Ileodictyon cibarius* section of 'egg': *p*, outer peridium, *j*, layer of jelly, *r*, folded receptacle, *g*, central gleba ($\times \frac{2}{3}$); (d) empty peridium ($\times \frac{2}{3}$); (e) expanded receptacle ($\times \frac{2}{3}$).

This appears to be a very reduced state of sexual behaviour, but at the same time all these organisms show the specialized feature of dikaryotic mycelium. One vegetative fusion is followed by the formation of an extremely large number of dikaryotic basidia with, consequently, a very large number of reduction divisions and the possibility of an enormous number of genetic variations within a single generation. In Basidiomycetes the dikaryotic stage of the life cycle has become the longest and thus the dominant phase while the haploid monokaryotic mycelium is short-lived.

The three distinct orders of higher Basidiomycetes which all have regular, single-celled basidia formed in an extensive hymenium or in an internally folded mass are clearly related, though it is not clear that any one order has been derived from any other. The Agaricales, which are far more numerous than the Gasteromycetales or the Aphyllophorales, appear to be the most successful group today. In all forest regions they form a conspicuous part of the vegetation and are known to be very important as soil micro-organisms and as mycorrhizal symbionts. As they are less readily isolated from the soil than the numerous Fungi Imperfecti less is known about the part they play in soil transformations.

The specialized sporophores produced by the higher Basidiomycetes are the largest and most complex structures formed by fungi, and it is the wide variety among them and their beauty which first attracts amateurs to the study of mycology. The broader aspects of the science involving the ecology and physiology of the organisms are of major importance, both concerning the control of species where they may be damaging, and in studying either the favourable changes they may bring about or possible uses which may be found for any of them.

Appendix

CLASSIFICATION SUMMARY

Living organisms are classified according to international rules, and according to a general scheme of supposed evolutionary relationship (Fig. A.1). Traditionally two 'kingdoms' were recognized, an animal kingdom for animals and a plant kingdom for all else. It has long been accepted that bacteria belong in one separate main *division*, rather isolated, and it is now generally thought that the fungi also are a separate main division for which the name Mycota has been suggested. This division includes separate *classes* with names ending in -mycetes, each of which may be divided into sub-classes with names ending in -mycetidae.

For all divisions of organisms each class is divided into a number of *orders* given names ending in -ales. Each order contains a number of *families*, with names ending in -aceae, each of which normally consists of a number of *genera* which are assumed to be related. Each genus usually comprises a number of closely related *species*. Each individual true-breeding kind of organism is a species which is given its genus and species name, and also its validating description, written in Latin, which is still in this respect an international language in science. Being Latin these names are customarily printed in italics or written underlined. Where any of the recognized groups are too large or too diverse they are divided into sub-groups such as sub-orders or sub-families.

For bacteria and fungi outline classifications, culled from the current standard works, are given below in sufficient detail to make a taxonomic framework for the organisms mentioned in this book.

OUTLINE CLASSIFICATION

BACTERIA

In the past bacteria were named primarily according to cell shape, of which there are three distinct types:

1. *Coccus*: simple minute spheres.
2. *Bacillus*: simple rigid rods, straight or slightly curved.
3. *Spirillum*: strongly curved rods.

Fig. A.1   Indication of possible relationships of living organisms.

The cell form is still a useful character in classification, but as a very large number of bacteria are recognized many more facts must be considered to make a workable scheme. A more natural grouping has been attempted based on all possible characters including the physiology of the species. An outline of the currently accepted scheme is given below.

EU-BACTERIA or TRUE BACTERIA comprise two orders:

1. **Pseudomonadales**

Rigid rod-shaped bacteria, polar-flagellate when motile, all Gram-negative.

Thiorhodaceae. Photosynthetic purple sulphur bacteria which contain bacteriochlorophyll and carotenoids.

Athiorhodaceae. Photosynthetic purple and brown non-sulphur bacteria.

Nitrobacteraceae. Chemosynthetic, deriving energy from oxidizing NH_3 or NO_2.

Pseudomonadaceae. Mostly soil and water organisms, many producing pigments. Several cause plant diseases. *Acetobacter* spp. are important in vinegar making. *Photobacterium* spp. are luminescent marine organisms often coating dead fish with a greenish glow.

Spirillaceae. Rigid, curved or spiral cells. *Vibrio* spp. are common soil organisms often seen in cultures and one, *V. cholerae*, is a serious pathogen which causes Asiatic cholera. *Cellfalcicula* spp. decompose cellulose in soil.

2. **Eubacteriales**

Simple rigid spherical or rod-shaped cells which are readily stained. If motile, with peritrichous flagella.

Azotobacteraceae. Large oval soil organisms capable of fixing N in culture when well supplied with carbohydrates.

Rhizobiaceae. Rhizobium spp. grow in legume root nodules which then fix N.

Entobacteriaceae. Active aerobic fermenters of carbohydrates. Many saprophytes and some important plant parasites. *Escherichia coli* grows in such enormous numbers in the gut of mammals that its presence in water supplies can be used as an indicator of faecal or sewage contamination. *Erwinia* spp. cause dry rots and galls of plants. *Pectobacterium* spp., which produce active pectinase enzymes, cause soft rots of plant tissues.

Brucellaceae. Obligate parasites often in warm-blooded animals. Have special growth requirements.

Micrococcaceae. Tiny spheres sometimes sticking together in masses, tetrads or packets. *Micrococcus* spp., which are often in tetrads, are common saprophytes and relatively harmless parasites; *Staphylococcus* spp., which are often in irregular clusters, frequently produce yellow pigments. Some are pathogenic.

Lactobacillaceae. Ferment sugars to lactic acid. *Streptococcus* spp. grow in chains and cause many human and animal diseases.

Corynebacteriaceae. Rods which often have a barred appearance. Some are saprophytes, others parasites or pathogens of animals or plants. Some such as *Corynebacterium diphtheriae* produce powerful exotoxins.

Bacillaceae. Characteristically produce endospores. Many are pathogenic to man. *Bacillus* spp. are aerobic. *B. anthracis* causes anthrax. *Clostridium* spp. are anaerobic and may produce powerful exotoxins; e.g. *Cl. tetani* causes tetanus and *Cl. botulinum* causes botulism.

The following orders stand apart from the first two and from one another.

3. Actinomycetales

Rod-shaped cells which stick together end to end in filaments which may even branch, thus resembling minute fungi. Most are saprophytes common in soil. A few are plant and animal parasites. Many produce substances inhibitory to other micro-organisms, some of which are used as antibiotics.

Mycobacteriaceae. Includes *Mycobacterium tuberculosis* which causes human tuberculosis.
Actinomycetaceae. Some species may reproduce by budding as well as by fission.
Streptomycetaceae. The filamentous form is well developed, and the tips of the filaments may divide repeatedly, the separate cells then rounding off to form spores.

4. Chlamydobacteriales or Filamentous Iron Bacteria

The filaments are formed by the bacterial sheaths which contain rows of separate rod-shaped cells. These grow by oxidizing ferrous compounds to ferric oxide which is deposited in the sheath. The rusty mass formed from these growths is often conspicuous in bogs and swamps, where in some cases it has accumulated sufficiently to form, or contribute to the formation of, bog iron ore. In iron water mains, particularly where the water has a noticeable iron content, species of *Sphaerotilus* (*Leptothrix*) form solid nodules which may build up till the pipe is blocked.

5. Beggiatoales or Filamentous Sulphur Bacteria

These are chemosynthetic bacteria which derive energy from oxidation of sulphides and then use CO_2 to build up carbohydrates. They grow in filaments with sheaths in which granules of sulphur are deposited. *Beggiatoa* spp. are examples of this group.

6. Myxobacteriales or Slime Bacteria

The cells of these are not rigid like those of the previous orders, but are flexible and capable of gliding movements. A whole mass of cells may move together and may collect in a large globule to form a fruiting body in which some of the cells form microcysts. They are common soil saprophytes. *Cytophaga* spp. and *Sporocytophaga* spp. produce cellulase enzymes which readily digest cellulose.

7. Spirochaetales

These are long, slender, coiled flexible cells which move actively though they have no flagella.

Spirochaetaceae. Very long cells up to 500 μ in length though only about 0·1 μ thick. Mainly free-living saprophytes and a few relatively harmless parasites.
Trepanemataceae. Much shorter cells up to 16 μ long. Many parasites causing serious diseases. *Trepanema pallidum* is the germ of syphilis and *T. pertenue* causes the disease yaws in the tropics.

8. Mycoplasmatales or pleuropneumonia organisms

Disease-causing parasites which have been isolated and grown in culture when they form minute delicate colonies of extremely pleomorphic organisms, comprising granules, cocci, rods and filaments in a cytoplasmic matrix, all lacking a rigid cell wall. Viable units readily pass through fine filters. These organisms are similar to the L-forms of true bacteria so it has been suggested that they may have originated from such bacteria.

9. Rickettsiales

These are obligate parasites similar in form to bacteria but only one-quarter to one-third the size being just visible with the light microscope. Very fine filters retain them though they are pleomorphic. They have been grown in cell tissue cultures and in chick embryos but not outside living cells. Rodents and such arthropods as fleas and lice commonly carry them, remaining unaffected by them, but if they are transmitted to man they may cause serious disease. *Rickettsia prowazekii*, which causes typhus, is the most notorious member of the group. Though these organisms are close to the larger true viruses they differ from them in having a more cellular type of organization and in being susceptible to some antibiotics.

Orders of uncertain affinity combining fungal and simple animal characters:

1. **Acrasiales** or Cellular Slime Moulds.

2. **Myxomycetes** or Mycetozoa

   Stemonitis spores in black masses on a stalked fructification with a well-developed capillitium.

3. **Plasmodiophorales.** *Plasmodiophora brassicae* causes clubroot of *Brassicas*.

FUNGI OR MYCOTA

Traditionally the first class of fungi was called the *Phycomycetes*, so named from a supposed relationship with algae. It is generally agreed now that the Phycomycetes include separate groups only distantly related, which are better treated as classes.

Class I   *Chytridiomycetes*

The fungi of this group have motile cells with a single posterior whiplash flagellum.

1. **Chytridiales**, chytrids. Simple unicells, in some cases with a few basal hyphae, mostly aquatic, saprophytic or parasitic.

   Synchytrium endobioticum causes wart disease of potatoes.
   Olpidium species are common parasites in roots.
   Chytridium species are common parasites on algae.
   Asterophlyctis species form a tiny thallus.

2. **Blastocladiales.** Thallus with distinct vegetative and reproductive parts, forming zoospores or motile gametes which may be either equal or differing in size.

   Blastocladiella, Allomyces.

3. **Monoblepharidales.** Thallus of coenocytic mycelium which forms zoospores or motile male gametes and large sessile oospheres which develop to form oospores.

   Monoblepharis.

7*

Class II   *Oomycetes*

Motile cells with one tinsel flagellum directed forwards and a whiplash flagellum directed backwards. Coenocytic mycelium bearing gametangia; fertilization of oospheres followed by formation of large oospores.

4. **Saprolegniales.** Water moulds, mostly saprophytic.

Saprolegnia.

5. **Peronosporales.** Saprophytic or parasitic fungi including many important plant pathogens, terrestrial but growing under damp conditions.

Pythium. The species of this genus include many important facultative parasites. The simple mycelium produces the reproductive cells; zoospores generally formed.

Phytophthora. Somewhat specialized plant parasites forming sporangia on special sporangiophores. Either zoospores are formed or sporangia behave as conidia.

P. infestans causes potato blight. *P. nicotianae* and its var. *parasitica* and other species attack plants causing destructive collar and root rots.

Plasmopara viticola, the vine downy mildew, causes serious losses in European vineyards; sporangia germinate to liberate zoospores.

Peronospora. Obligate parasites causing downy mildews. Specialized sporangiophores bear sporangia which typically behave as conidia. *P. parasitica* commonly attacks crucifers.

Bremia lactucae causes downy mildew of lettuces.

Albugo species are obligate parasites causing the white blister rusts of many kinds of plants. *A. candida* infects crucifers. Sporangiophores bearing chains of sporangia form under the leaf epidermis which finally bursts open. Sporangia germinate to produce zoospores.

Class III   *Zygomycetes*

No motile cells. Coenocytic hyphae somewhat or considerably differentiated; aerial sporangiophores bearing sporangia with many spores, or, in some, conidiophores bear conidia. Multinucleate gametangia equal or differing somewhat in size.

1. **Mucorales.** Rapidly-growing coarse coenocytic hyphae, homothallic or heterothallic, mostly saprophytes, a few parasites.

Mucor, Rhizopus, Pilobolus, Endogone.

2. **Entomophthorales.** Mostly parasitic on insects; forming conidia.

Class IV   *Ascomycetes*

Sexual spores borne internally in a sac-like ascus.

Sub-class A   *Hemiascomycetidae*

Asci formed singly. Growth by budding.

1. **Endomycetales.** Yeasts, specialized unicells.

Saccharomyces, a large genus including a number of economically important species and varieties or sub-species.

Schizosaccharomyces, fission yeasts.

2. **Taphrinales**. Specialized parasites of higher plants, ascospores budding like yeast cells, hyphae formed in plant tissues, cultured growth yeast-like.

T. deformans causes peach leaf curl. *T. coerulescens* causes similar discoloured puckering of oak leaves.

Sub-class B *Euascomycetidae*

Ascogenous hyphae within a fruiting body, the **ascocarp**, usually bear many asci, each of which has a single wall.

3. **Plectascales**. Forming small enclosed globose ascocarps (**cleistothecia**), containing relatively small numbers of asci.

Eurotium, many common moulds (Aspergilli).
Erysiphe, powdery mildews, common obligate parasites.
Elaphomyces, forming tuber-like ascocarps underground.

4. **Sphaeriales**. Ascocarps flask-shaped structures opening by apical ostioles (**perithecia**).

Sordaria, many small coprophilous saprophytes.
Neurospora, widespread saprophytes commonly cultured experimentally.
Nectria, perithecia small, usually bright orange or pink. *N. cinnabarina* is a common saprophyte while the similar *Dialonectria galligena* causes apple canker.
Gibberella, perithecia small, scattered, dark-coloured. *G. fujikuroi* is the source of the important hormone, gibberellic acid. *G. macrolopha* causes stem cankers on some New Zealand shrubs.
Xylosphaera, perithecia embedded in a dark-coloured stroma. *X. hypoxylon* and *X. polymorpha* commonly produce black fructifications on rotting wood.
Daldinia concentrica, the common charcoal fungus.
Ceratostomella ulmi, causing Dutch elm disease, produces smooth carbonaceous perithecia.

5. **Clavicipitales**. Asci in small perithecia embedded in a stalked stroma; ascospores thread-like.

Claviceps purpurea forms ergot of grain.
Cordyceps species parasitize larvae and nymphs of many insects forming vegetable caterpillars.

6. **Helotiales**. Asci inoperculate, in a hymenium exposed on discs or in cups (**apothecia**). A large and diverse order.

Geoglossum, *Mitrula* and *Leotia* are common terrestrial species with stalked stromata with hymenium spreading over the head.
Sclerotinia, forming stalked apothecia from a stroma, and *Monilinia*, forming similar apothecia from mummified fruit, include important plant pathogens.
Bulgaria and *Coryne* include a number of saprophytes forming gelatinous apothecia on rotting wood.
Helotium includes many saprophytic species forming brightly coloured discs on rotting wood. *H. epiphyllum* with bright orange-yellow discs is common.
Chlorociboria (Chlorosplenium) aeruginascens, the green staining fungus, is often seen on and in fallen wood.
Diplocarpon rosae is the common parasite causing black spot of rose leaves.

7. **Phacidiales.** Plant parasites which form apothecia immersed in the host tissues which split open above a mature apothecium.

Rhytisma acerinum causes tar spot of the leaves of *Acer* species.

8. **Pezizales.** Ascocarps large, bright or light-coloured apothecia; asci opening by a lid or operculum. Many have sculptured or ornamented spores.

Morchella, morels, and *Helvella* have large stalked fructifications.
Peziza and *Aleuria* have large cup-shaped apothecia.
Cyttaria species are obligate parasites causing woody galls on *Nothofagus* species.

9. **Tuberales,** truffles. Fructifications formed underground, some with large swollen asci and large sculptured spores.

Tuber and *Elaphomyces* species may be found by digging in woods.

Sub-class C   *Loculoascomycetidae*

Asci, all with double walls, are formed in small enclosed fruiting bodies. Many are saprophytes, some are important plant parasites.

10. **Dothidiales.** Many sooty mould fungi are represented in this order.

Euryachora ulmi and *E. betulina* commonly form black spots on dead elm or birch leaves.
Mycosphaerella species cause black spots on leaves of many plants, e.g. *M. fragariae* on strawberries, *M. lineolata* on dead grasses.

11. **Pleosporales** includes a large number of species which form asci in perithecia.

Venturia includes many species causing dark spots on fruits or leaves; e.g. *V. inaequalis*, the fungus of apple scab.
Ophiobolus species grow as saprophytes or parasites on herbaceous roots and stems forming perithecia on the dead stems.

Class V   *Basidiomycetes*

Sexual spores developed externally on a basidium.

Sub-class A   *Heterobasidiomycetidae*

Basidium septate or deeply divided; basidiospores often budding.

1. **Ustilaginales.** Smut fungi, highly specialized plant parasites, some of economic importance.

Ustilago species cause loose smuts of many plants.
Tilletia caries or *T. foetida* causes bunt, or stinking or covered smut of wheat.

2. **Uredinales.** Rust fungi, numerous highly specialized, obligate parasites often with complex life histories involving alternate plant hosts.

Puccinia graminis causes black stem rust of grain.
P. malvacearum causes hollyhock rust.
Cronartium ribicola causes rust of *Ribes* and five-needled pines.

3. **Tremellales** (together with the related orders **Auriculariales** and **Dacryomycetales**) form small to large fruiting bodies of a gelatinous texture with an extensive layer of hymenium.

Auricularia auricula, Jew's ear fungus.

Calocera viscosa, a common orange-yellow slimy fungus, is shaped like a *Clavaria* but is of different texture.

Sub-class B *Homobasidiomycetidae*

Basidium a single, large clavate cell bearing four basidiospores on four apical sterigmata.

4. **Aphyllophorales.** A large order of species with a hymenium which is smooth, wrinkled, toothed or poroid, borne on variously shaped sporophores.

Clavaria, club fungi; many common saprophytic species.

Sparassis crispa somewhat resembles a fragile cauliflower.

Stereum species form thin brackets with a smooth hymenial surface. *S. hirsutum* is a common saprophyte, *S. purpureum* a common parasite.

Serpula lacrymans, a destructive saprophyte of timber.

Cantharellus cibarius, chanterelle, and *Craterellus cornucopioides*, both good edible species; form irregular funnel-shaped sporophores.

Hydnum repandum has large toothed sporophores.

Polyporus, *Phaeolus*, *Trametes*, form small to large annual bracket sporophores, fleshy or corky.

Ganoderma and *Fomes* form large woody perennial brackets.

5. **Agaricales.** Fleshy toadstools with the hymenium developed on gills or in soft pores.

Amanita with white spores has both volva and ring.

Armillaria with white spores has decurrent gills and a ring on the tough stem.

Lepiota with free gills has white spores and a ring on the stem.

Russula and *Lactarius* with white amyloid sculptured spores have neither ring nor volva.

Agaricus with dark purple-brown spores has a well-developed ring.

Coprinus with black spores has deliquescing gills.

Boletus forms large, stalked, spongy sporophores with pores.

6. **Gasteromycetales.** The sporophore at first is enclosed completely in a more or less rounded peridium which may break open to expose the internally formed spores. The different families of this order are not very closely related.

Lycoperdon, puff-balls, opening by a pore.

Geastrum, earth stars, have an outer peridial wall opening to form a star, containing an inner peridium like a puff-ball.

Calvatia, very large puff-ball, opening only by the decay of the peridium.

Sphaerobolus, tiny ball-shaped peridia dehisce and shoot out peridiola containing the spores.

Crucibulum, bird's nest fungi, contain egg-like peridiola.

Phallus, stinkhorn, forms a gelatinous sporophore.

Ileodictyon and *Aseroe* also form gelatinous receptacles.

Class V *Deuteromycetes* or *Fungi Imperfecti*

As only the asexual stages of these fungi are known they are classified according to the form of their conidiophores and conidia.

1. **Sphaeropsidales.** Conidiophores produced inside small flask-shaped receptacles (pycnidia). Many plant parasites.

Phoma, Septoria. S. apii causes leaf spot of celery, a serious plant disease.

2. **Melanconiales.** Conidiophores in small, more or less disc-shaped masses which break through the surface of leaves and other substrata forming *acervuli*. Many plant parasites commonly attacking leaves and stems.

Gloeosporium, Colletotrichum, Marssonina. M. panattoniana causes anthracnose of lettuce.

3. **Moniliales** or **Hyphales.** Mycelium bearing free, erect conidiophores which produce conidia usually by budding. This is much the largest order.

Penicillium, Aspergillus, Botrytis, Cladosporium, Fusarium, Monilia, Arthrobotrys.

Sporobolomyces and *Tilletiopsis*, the mirror yeasts, common leaf epiphytes producing very abundant air-borne conidia.

Microsporum and *Trichophyton*, dermatophytes.

4. **Mycelia Sterilia.** No spores formed but many form sclerotia.

Rhizoctonia, Sclerotium.

Bibliography

BACTERIA

CRUICKSHANK, R. (1965) *Medical Microbiology*. Livingstone, Edinburgh and London.
FRY, B. A. (1955) *The Nitrogen Metabolism of Micro-organisms*. Methuen, London.
GALE, E. F. (1959) *Synthesis and Organisation in the Bacterial Cell*. Wiley, New York; Chapman and Hall, London.
GILLIES, R. R. and DODDS, T. C. (1965) *Bacteriology Illustrated*. Livingstone, Edinburgh and London.
KLEINEBERGER-NOBEL, E. (1965) *Focus on Bacteria*. Academic Press, New York and London.
OCINSKY, O. L. and UMBREIT, W. W. (1959) *An Introduction to Bacterial Physiology*. Freeman, San Francisco and London.

FUNGI

AINSWORTH, G. C. (1963) *A Dictionary of the Fungi*. Commonwealth Mycological Institute, Kew.
—— (1966) A General Purpose Classification of Fungi. *Biblphy. syst. Mycol.*, **1**, 1–4.
ALEXOPOULOS, C. J. (1962) *Introductory Mycology*. Wiley, New York and London.
BESSEY, E. A. (1950) *Morphology and Taxonomy of Fungi*. Blakiston, Philadelphia and Toronto.
BURNETT, J. H. (1968) *Fundamentals of Mycology*. Arnold, London.
DENNIS, R. W. G. (1960) *British Cup Fungi*. Ray Society, London.
FINCHAM, J. R. S. (1965) *Microbial and Molecular Genetics*. English University Press, London.
FINCHAM, J. R. S. and DAY, P. R. (1965) *Fungal Genetics*. Blackwell, Oxford.
GÄUMANN, E. (1965) *Die Pilze*. Birkhäuser, Basel and Stuttgart.
HAWKER, L. E. (1950) *Physiology of Fungi*. Clarendon Press, Oxford.
—— (1957) *The Physiology of Reproduction in Fungi*. University Press, Cambridge.

INGOLD, C. T. (1953) *Dispersal in Fungi*. Clarendon Press, Oxford.
—— (1961) *The Biology of Fungi*. Hutchinson, London.
INGRAM, M. (1955) *An Introduction to the Biology of Yeasts*. Pitman, London.
LANGE, M. and HORA, F. B. (1963) *Guide to Mushrooms and Toadstools*. Collins, London.
LANGERON, M. and VANBREUSEGHEM, R. (translated J. WILKINSON) (1965) *Outline of Mycology*. Pitman, London.
LARGE, E. C. (1940) *The Advance of the Fungi*. Cape, London.
MIDDLETON, J. T. (1943) On *Pythium*. *Mem. Torrey bot. Club*, **20**, 1.
RAMSBOTTOM, J. (1955) *Mushrooms and Toadstools*. Collins, London.
SINGER, R. (1962). *The Agaricales*. Cramer, Weinheim.
SPARROW, F. J. (1960) *Aquatic Phycomycetes*. University of Michigan Press, Ann Arbor.
WAKEFIELD, E. M. and DENNIS, R. W. G. (1950) *Common British Fungi*. Gawthorn, London.

LICHENS

HALE, M. E. (1967) *The Biology of Lichens*. Contemporary Biology series. Edward Arnold, London.

VIRUSES

BURNET, F. M. (1953) *Viruses and Man*. Penguin Books, London.
FRAENKEL-CONRAT, H. (1962) *Design and Function at The Threshold of Life: The Viruses*. Academic Press, New York and London.
SMITH, K. M. (1943) *Beyond the Microscope*. Penguin Books, London.
—— (1962) *Viruses*. Cambridge University Press, Cambridge.

PHYSIOLOGICAL ASPECTS

BALDWIN, E. (1957) *Dynamic Aspects of Biochemistry*. University Press, Cambridge.
BALDWIN, E. (1967) *The Nature of Biochemistry*. University Press, Cambridge.
BAYLISS, L. E. (1959) *Principles of General Physiology*. Longmans, London.
CASEY, E. J. (1962) *Biophysics*. Reinhold, New York.
DOWNES, HELEN (1955) *The Chemistry of Living Cells*. Longmans, London and New York.
FRUTON, J. S. and SIMMONDS, S. (1963). *General Biochemistry*. Wiley, New York.
HAWKER, L. E. *et al.* (1960) *An Introduction to the Biology of Micro-organisms*. Arnold, London.
RAMSAY, J. A. (1965) *The Experimental Basis of Modern Biology*. University Press, Cambridge.

APPLIED ASPECTS

BOYCE, J. S. (1938) *Forest Pathology*. McGraw-Hill, New York and Maidenhead.

Index

References to illustrations are shown by italic numbers